I Had to Die
to Learn How to Live

Alan R. Stevenson

© 2015 Alan R. Stevenson

All Rights Reserved.

No part of this publication may be reproduced, stored in a retrieval system, or transmitted, in any form or by any means, electronic, mechanical, photocopying, recording, or otherwise, without the written permission of the author.

First published by Dog Ear Publishing
4011 Vincennes Rd
Indianapolis, IN 46268
www.dogearpublishing.net

ISBN: 978-1-4575-4346-3

This book is printed on acid-free paper.

Printed in the United States of America

> **"Our Greatest Time,
> is often
> Our Hardest Moments"**
>
> —*Alan R. Stevenson*

One of the more important realizations I wish for you by the end of this book is to...

"Remember: That each one of us is an individual cell of the Human Race"

The bond for us all is there and the time is here to realize the foundation of "Being" and the need to unite as a single body.

Dedication

To all those who I know, as well as to those I do not. With special thanks to Dana O. Crandell who brought this book from the non-physical into the physical.

Contents

Preface ix

1 *The Day I Stood at Heaven's Door* 1

2 *A Stretch in Time* 14

3 *My Point to Begin* 29

4 *Your Point to Begin* 37

5 *The Science of Reality* 49

6 *The Spark of All There Is* 57

7 *From Here to There* 76

8 *E = M* 84

9 *The Art of Being What I've Learned* 94

10	*Frankenstein Syndrome*	*108*
11	*Architects We Are*	*116*
12	*Life's GPS*	*124*
13	*Seeing the Future from Here*	*129*
14	*Of the Heart From the Heart*	*134*
15	*The Inescapable*	*141*
16	*Walking the Journey*	*150*
17	*Messages from 111*	*163*

Preface

NDE's, also known as near-death experiences, have been written about for some time, and seem to be more commonplace today. There are several commonalities from one experience to another, the most prominent being how profoundly and permanently changed those who have experienced them have become. Another is the need for a post-experience adjustment period after having had a glimpse into what we all fear at one time or another, due to a lack of understanding. Being given the chance to step to the other side, however, has aided us in the "dot connecting" process. This out-of-sync, sideways step from physical "reality" and the norm can be likened to being shown how a magician's trick or illusion was done. Initially, watching the illusion happens from one perspective. Once the secret is disclosed, however, an individual's previous perception falls away, having been replaced with a completely different perspective thereafter. Beliefs and loose concepts about life and death, living and dying prior to the NDE disassemble, extending the adjustment period.

The material within these pages is not so much about a near-death experience in the same manner as others have written, as I have felt, since that fateful day, a strong need to write more about what was truly important. I needed to accomplish this as I worked my way through the dot connecting adjustment period, then find a way in which to live according to the lessons learned from having died.

If we can learn what is truly important in regard to our conscious as well as physical existence, then understand what we truly are at our foundation, we come to fully realize the potential of our innate abilities, moving us towards the truth.

Life, living, being and dying are connective processes, whether we are merely getting through our day, with all that that may entail, or driving from New York to Los Angeles. During the journey, there are points or dots we connect in succession, telling us upon arrival that we are on track. As children, we learn through this very process, moving on to the next point after arriving at each one. For example, we learn at a young age that ten plus ten equals twenty, though not before learning one plus one equals two, creating a greater depth of understanding.

Since accepting the task I have spent a great deal of time connecting the dots of all that happened and all that was shown to me. It is my challenge to relay that ever-so-important knowledge in the simplest dot-connected-to-dot manner possible.

One of the lessons learned while "in the foyer" of the other side is that we are all given a choice at that point of whether to move on from this physical life. Make no mistake in thinking that coming back is not moving on, for myself as well as many others have been unequivocally changed for evermore. You see it all the time. This is the exact reason that accident victims, as well as those who fall victim to physical illness survive and come back when from a medical perspective they should not have. Those individuals chose to return here at that same pivotal moment. More important, though is that in physical life, where you have been, where you are, where you are going, what you are doing and who you have become have all been a matter of choice! The path you walk today and even the one you tread tomorrow will be of your own choosing. The choice and the ability to choose belongs to us and us alone - though what drives that choice at times can be odd at best.

The factors within the equation that affect that are exactly what this book is about.

The truth is, no one, not a single soul past or present was born with or arrived here on earth with a hand manual or guide of how to drive this vehicle through the complicated maze called Life. We have, for far too long, been bumping and banging our way along since the beginning in a chaotic dance that more closely resembles bumper cars at a county fair than anything else.

Once you understand how the physical reality in which we live operates, as well as what we are all governed by, and come to understand the "why", you truly become your own master.

The truth about life, living, dying and death itself is so incredibly far removed from our perception. This due largely to good intentions by so many who want to help bring about the change we all internally yearn for. I judge no one for I cannot. As you will hopefully learn, not a single being has the right to judge another, for no one is slightly less or remotely more than another soul, regardless of the situation or appearance. The physical world's societal norm has taught and built such a closed-in, mistrustful norm of existence that we are struggling with learning to listen to and believe in ourselves. Don't fill your mind with thoughts of "maybe". Feel that which you truly are and be that Being.

I am who I am and have had an event come about in my life that helped show me what I am. That has made all the difference....

CHAPTER 1

The Day I Stood at Heaven's Door

"After coming back, I fell in Love with all that there is, from all that I had learned."

—Alan R. Stevenson

I wish I could say the day I died was just another ordinary day so it would appear more literarily dramatic. Instead, like an ironic preview of coming attractions, the day was besieged by the only snowstorm of the winter season in the Niagara Peninsula. For me, it was a prelude to the inevitable reality that each of us will someday face. It is a day that some consider while others fear it to an extreme.

February 26, 2010, is only a short distance behind me now that I've spent some time in the sun amongst the care of loved ones. I am grateful for having had a peaceful space to do my healing of body, mending of mind, sorting of soul and learning the lessons of what "Being" means.

That morning was quite different in that the fabric of my physical world appeared somewhat out of sync. Under ordinary circumstances, most would be oblivious to these minute details. Pain from what I assumed was severe heartburn had lingered for three days. I was driven by a less than ideal life situation, ignoring the pain although I knew deep down I shouldn't. It was here I first stepped into the conflicting pothole, having prioritized work over my health. I got ready for work, my routine unchanged except for the sluggishness that dogged me as I put on my winter boots.

Seized with a powerful sense of apprehension at venturing out into the bitter-cold Canadian weather, I still ignored the instincts that relentlessly nagged me. Thanks to a financial crisis where ends already did not meet and a work schedule that had me off for the previous six days, I was compelled to ignore my inner voice and layer up to deal with the harsh weather. What my internal voice couldn't convince me of, the increasing pain of even the simplest movement began to. The thought of walking six blocks in the snow storm only worsened my physical discomfort. For a fleeting moment, I thought of asking my younger brother for help, as he was in the living room watching the morning news.

Unfortunately, I had already envisioned his typical, "Suck it up buttercup," response to anyone mentioning a personal problem or hardship of any nature. Quickly dismissing the thought, I pulled my coat over my bulky layers and with a sense of great sadness, slipped my hat and gloves on.

Even as I opened the door to a blizzard and freezing temperatures, the sense of my impending doom hovered on the fringe of my awareness. The inexplicable sadness began to overwhelm me and the raw emotion was yet another warning.

Ignoring it with stoicism, I simply stepped outside and closed the door to the first opportunity to save my life. I didn't say anything to my brother, not even a simple goodbye, as tension was still high following an argument two days earlier, the cause as trivial as most were.

The blasting wind and snow intensified, clutching the collar of my coat to my cheek as I cleared the steps of the front porch. I churned my feet through the foot-deep snow, making my way over to the main street. With my head bowed, the biting winds still teared up my eyes. Even in optimal health, walking across town as I usually did wasn't an option on such a brutal day. The agony in my chest had reached a disorienting level so I stopped at the store around the corner to grab a roll of antacid tablets, though it was against my better judgment. I simply knew I needed some kind of relief at that point - hell, anything!

While waiting behind another customer paying for their purchases, the store clerk, whom I knew fairly well, glanced at me several times with concern. Once again, an opportunity to save my life was presenting itself, if I would simply have asked for help. There was no excuse. I'd had many conversations with the clerk over the past six months and knew that he had been a paramedic back in his native Serbia. He had been unable to qualify as a paramedic in Canada due to his English. The sad and ironic thing about that, was his English was better than most born here.

His eyes never left me as I struggled to open the antacid roll. I barely remember paying for them, and as he counted the change, his eyes carefully assessed me.

"Are you all right?"

"Oh, I'm okay."

"You don't look too well," he said more firmly.

Though his words registered in my pain-wracked mind, denial fought me on every front of my deteriorating condition, challenging all my common sense.

"I'll be all right.", I insisted, though in truth a feeling of sheer dismay coupled with an emotional hopelessness had my thoughts flitting and flirting. All the while, the emotional roller coaster sped up to the point where it felt as though it would come off the tracks at any moment.

Concentrating on the antacid package, was all I could do to keep it together. Finally succeeding, I headed for the door while popping several tablets into my mouth. The regularly simple task of pushing open the door was as overwhelming as pushing a car, and once again I sidestepped an opportunity to save my life.

I stepped out into the ferocious storm to walk six blocks through weather conditions I had not seen in years. Dragging my feet like lead weights, as it was all but impossible to lift them from the steadily deepening snow. With each step, the vise of dismay tightened its grip on my chest even further. My mind searched for solutions within the pain-induced fog, as my ego barged to the surface of my thoughts and screamed, "This isn't the day and nothing's going to happen to me!"

Struggling down Lake Street just past the armories, I looked around to determine how far I was from the bus stop and realized in heart sinking fashion that I was completely alone in the storm. There wasn't a single soul to be seen anywhere, no cars, no people, no businesses open, only the bone-chilling wind, driving snow and excruciating pain. I felt more alone than I had ever felt or truly been before. To this day, I still clearly remember my instincts shouting, "You need to get to the hospital!" I persisted in the foolish belief that if I could just keep on keeping on, the episode would pass and I might be okay after all.

Making it to the bus stop felt like a victory, though now I had to wait for the delayed bus. When it arrived and I boarded, I slipped the coins into the slot, and realized as it lurched away into the snow that everything had changed from one heartbeat to the next. I sagged into a seat a couple back behind the driver, becoming severally diaphoretic (sweating profusely) at this point. My ability to physically move was reduced to slow motion, as my hands wouldn't obey my struggles to remove my gloves, coat and hat. With a grim understanding, I knew I had no choice but to ask for help now or die, and even with the cold truth staring me in the face, I couldn't immediately bring myself to act. Once again my instincts screamed at me to ask for help. Who knew how the mind and body truly acted under duress until faced with the most dire circumstances?

Without thought, as the bus drivers eyes met mine within the mirror that hung above her, I asked her to call 911. She asked only why as she picked up the on-board phone. In a faltering voice I told her I was having a heart attack. Turning slowly, I noticed a woman sitting across from me. A horrified expression filled her round face as she clutched her bulky purse tightly to her chest.

The pain began dissipating rapidly as a serene peacefulness gently enveloped me. My gaze slowly lowered to my boots, and I thought, "So this is what it's like to die." During that transitory thought, I died. My vision winked into darkness as all the pain I had suffered over the past three days vanished without worry, anxiety or fear. The calm peacefulness strengthened, replacing all the pain of the moments before.

Then slowly, a misty opening began to appear about six inches or so in diameter in front of me. My mind was clear and I felt light as air, as a strong sense of fascination engulfed my being as I felt a slow, easy, sideways movement with only the slightest pressure around me. Glancing down, I noticed that I had four arms, legs, hands and feet. One set was more densely proportioned while the other sets were translucent appendages hovering just outside my physical body.

At this point, my long-time guardian, a tiger nearly six feet tall at the shoulder, stepped out of the near-blizzard conditions onto the bus. It seemed odd, but I knew him from other encounters during my life. Tiger is a soul guardian or what is known as 'a protector of souls.' He approached me and lovingly rubbed his head on the left side of my face. Slowly drawing back, he looked into my eyes and spoke in my mind.

You are about to die.

Turning his head toward the adjacent windows, where holographic images displayed events from the past, present, and future, showing the images of my two daughters, Meaghan and Danika

He looked back at me and said, *If you choose to.*

"So I have a choice?" I asked in confusion.

Yes, you do. All of you have a choice. Everyone is given a choice with no judgment passed either way. Where you have been, where you are, and where you are going at all times is of your own choice.

I was overwhelmed by an emotional summary of my life, which we must all experience for a few moments, whether staying or coming back. The best way to describe it would be to take every thought and feeling you've ever had, and physical action you've ever done, then place it all into one emotional category. Ask yourself which emotion best sums up your life to date. Mine was marked by guilt for wasting my many talents and, in turn, my life.

We both gazed deeply into each others' eyes and in a soft, submissive tone I replied,

"I want to stay. I want to live."

Very well Tiger said. *Now you have a task.*

Tiger turned to leave as the thought flowed freely to me to follow. I didn't actually get up or walk anywhere, but we instantly traveled far to a place shrouded in a luminous, white mist.

As we arrived, Tiger stepped ahead of me, turning to face me at an angle. Out on the fringe of my left peripheral vision, three Beings appeared, whom I've come to refer to as the Beings of 111 or 3. Once I focused my attention on them, they vanished, but when I looked at Tiger, they reappeared, only to vanish once again as I turned toward them. It reminded me of gazing at a distant faint star in the night sky. If you look directly at it, it seems to wink out of sight, but reappears if you look a bit off and away from it.

Here began my first lesson with Tiger. I was emotionally searching for understanding as to why I could, yet couldn't, see the three Beings. *It does not matter*, Tiger whispered. He then informed me the central Being was a Teacher, not only to myself, but to the other two Beings present. Eventually, they will become teachers themselves. The Teacher is an original consciousness (or child if you prefer) of what most refer to as God.

At this point, there are some important details readers must understand. First, time as we perceive it does not exist. It is but a way in which to measure distance, such as the distance light travels in a year, or the sun traversing the sky from horizon to horizon. For point of reference sake, however, we shall stick with time as it is traditionally understood. I died at roughly 9:25am and was about to spend what would be considered a day's worth of time on the other side, prior to coming back to physical reality roughly ten minutes later, at 9:35am.

I was soon to understand the purpose of coming to this place as my focus intensified to such an extreme level that I felt anything and everything was possible. Tiger acted as the conduit for what was to follow as most of it flowed through him. A little to my right, several holographic, free flowing images with full background appeared. Several times during the projection of images I would lack a clear understanding of the point being made. I would say in my mind *Yes, but* ...At which point Tiger would patiently exclaim, *It does not matter.* Finally, I began to understand that phrase was an important teaching tool as well a learning one. There are things that truly are important, and then there are those that simply are not. The point at which you learn to make that distinction will free you to become the Being you were always meant to be.

Tiger escorted me back to the bus, as it was time for me to return. I thanked him for sharing their insights and truths with me. He once again rubbed his head against mine with intense love before turning and leaving the bus. I haven't seen nor sensed him in any way since that moment he slinked his way off the bus.

As my physical reality started to return I saw the bus driver standing before me distraught and exclaiming, "What can I do? I think he's dead!"

With my physical reality returning to me, I became fully aware of the pain and surrounding environment. The first paramedic stepped onto the bus and asked a few questions to assess my condition. I felt incredibly relieved that someone had finally come to help me. When he turned and left the bus, I was filled with such dread that I screamed in my mind, "Please don't leave me now," but he was only returning to the ambulance to retrieve more equipment. The bus driver waited beside me until the paramedics returned. A frenzy of activity ensued while three of them worked to stabilize me enough to transport me to the hospital.

At St. Catharines General Hospital, a doctor and nurse proceeded to inject, spray, and administer a vast amount of medication, once the severity of my biological condition had been diagnosed. Then came the frantic orders from the trauma doctor, "Go! Go! Go! Get him out of here now!" Off I went to the more distant Hamilton General for heart surgery to save my life. It was a straight run down the Queen's Highway, the journey hastened by the urgent sirens on what would have otherwise been at least a thirty-minute drive. Through the windows of the rear door, I watched cars vanish as though they were standing still, and I realized how fast we were traveling.

The nurse sitting beside me looked at both paramedics flanking me and said, "We don't want to alarm you as you need to stay as calm as you can," then glancing at the cellphone on my lap, she added, "but if you wish to call someone, now would be the time to do that."

My eyes welled up as I admitted that my cellphone had been disconnected the day before. She quickly retrieved hers and asked for a number to dial for me. I mentally searched for the first choice to call, but at the same time I didn't want to upset anyone. That was one of the hardest decisions I had to make, but I knew my daughters needed to know how much I loved them and what they had meant to me during the time they had shared my life.

Giving the nurse their mother's number at work, she tapped each number on the keypad as I struggled to remember it, then she passed the phone to me. Once Deb answered, I immediately apologized and explained the situation, then I relayed the message she needed to hear from me. I also told her that although things had not worked out as we had planned many years before, I cared deeply for her and would continue to do so no matter what ultimately happened to me, and let her go with a deep sense of love. I envisioned the stoic expression on her face that would have concealed her distress, but I really had no idea what transpired in those few moments after I hung up.

When we arrived at the hospital, the paramedics rushed me through the blowing snow into the ER and down the hallways to an operating room. As I lay on the operating table, the OR staff stripped me down completely and prepped me for surgery.

While the prepping was going on a young looking surgeon approached and slightly leaning over me asked, "What the hell are you doing on my table?"

With my last ounce of quick wit, I said, "I'm having a bad day."

He smiled a little and walked away for a short time. When he returned, he said, "Your left artery is one-hundred percent blocked. Medically, you had no reason to have survived what's known as a "widow-maker" heart attack."

I looked at him intently (with an unintentional dreary gaze, considering all the chemicals that had been pumped into my body) , and calmly said, "Oh, but I do."

I slowly regained consciousness later on that day, emerging from a somewhat foggy state to a sense of calm peacefulness. A minor physical discomfort was still present, though only in the background of my awareness. Awaking in a large ICU room, it was there I began to realize and feel the magical sense of being alive and all the magic a day holds. Over the following week in the hospital, gifts that I had returned with became apparent. "Gifts" may be the wrong term, as they are merely innate abilities in all, but for me they were life-changing legacies of my experience.

Terri writes;

"I agree with your statement Alan about choice. I am where I am today because of the choices I have made. If I understand you correctly you say that your experience with death you were given a choice. I believe it to be that way. I say this because my daughter died last May. She had melanoma and was diagnosed far to late to save her. Anyhow, the prognosis was not in her favor. She was in the hospital only two weeks. On the last day of her life she was not verbally responsive her eyes were opened but rolled back into her head. I knew death was not

far away and my sister told me to tell her that it was okay to go because she was hanging on for her family. I knew she was right and with all the love in my heart I told her that it was alright to go home with the angels. I told her how much I loved her and spent what seemed like forever with her. I left the room and went downstairs with my youngest daughter. A few minutes into lunch my sister came and got us. Amanda had passed. She told me that she had been in the room with her dad and that the last thing she saw her do was to grab her dads' hand with tears streaming down her cheeks. Thank You ever so much Alan once again!"

CHAPTER 2

A Stretch of Time

> "My near death experience made me realize
> I was not who I could be or was meant to be,
> that I'm better than what I'd become or where I was."
>
> —Alan R. Stevenson

Andrea wrote to me to say;

"I am <u>soul</u> happy you survived to share your story. Just weeks ago I ended up in the ER with a blood clot in my heart. I thank the higher beings who consistently watch over me to allow me to breathe again to share my love and light with the world."

There exists with pretty much all NDE experiencers, a post experience period of being out of sync with physical reality. From the stories I've read, to the people I have talked with around the world, most go through those initial days, feeling somewhat lost. The disorienting feeling is more of a core sensation than a biological one, with an emotional origin. Since the inception of science and with the support of societal beliefs, there has not been a proper separation of these two entities. There is a significant difference between the biological glove and our emotions, wherein emotion is an aspect of what we truly are, as you shall see. Yes, there is the statement, "mind, body and soul", but it has become as indifferent as paint, metal and wheels are to a car. It is my sincere hope that in time you will come to truly understand that difference as well as it's significance.

A short while after the initial adjustment period, there comes a point where many begin trying to write it all down, either the old fashioned, hand-written way or by digital means. As for myself, I chose to use a pen and pencil, ending up with a very scattered notation format. Though we are trying to connect the dots, this process isn't so much for ourselves. We, for the most part, truly get it, due to having been on the other side. I've felt all along the actual reason behind it has more to do with explaining it to the loved ones around us. It is they who notice the significant change in *who* we are, as we have, more importantly, come to understand *what* we are. Notes are made and drawings are done in a vain attempt to pour it all out, though none of it actually comes close to touching the surface of all that was experienced. We try in various ways to express this new sense or feeling that wasn't a part of who we were prior to the experience. I, myself haven't been able to create any drawings of it, nor have I seen a single artist's picture, painting or drawing that touched its loving beauty. Nevertheless, a driving force within each of us tries to mesh the contradictory nature of the two states of reality we have experienced.

This can go on for days to months and for a few, even years, regardless of the process, venue, or format chosen to capture the essence of the experience. There does, however remain a specific constant during this period, and that is one of a great, inexplicable calm – a loving peacefulness. During chaotic physical situations or extreme external emotional states, the peacefulness remains. Even though we are unable to express its total essence, the love we found, felt and touched within our true selves never leaves.

I'd been writing down the dot connecting while I implemented the lessons I learned from that day of February 26th 2010, such as "The only things of any true value are the moments we each have and what we do with them. This is a choice we must learn to make. Just as a palm full of coins that renews, we become lost in the spending, often finding a realization at the end that comes only too late for far too many." The important truths we are to learn are actually found within the minute aspects of the larger picture. The next time you gaze upon a very large tree, pay more attention to the branches, twigs, leaves and their veins, and even deeper within them. Always keep in mind that to build a puzzle you must first sort the pieces.

Jotting down notes here, there and on anything I could, I didn't start in earnest to organize them for this book till after March 16th 2014. That date ended up being every single bit as significant as the day I died. That weekend in March, I attended a Hay House conference at Roy Thompson Hall in Toronto to see, and hopefully meet, Anita Moorjani. Anita is the author of the book *Dying to be Me* by Hay House Publications. How I came to end up there was one of those "odd at best" moments, that's for sure.

During the early months of 2013 I dipped into a period of personal doubt in regard to what I was doing, the reasons why and whether I should even bother writing anymore of it down. These doubts originated from seeing and feeling so much distraught the world over. While clicking through various things on the internet one day, I stumbled on a video interview that Anita Moorjani recorded with Lilou Mace.

Now, at that time I didn't know anything about Anita, or even who she was. Still, something extremely strong within me, as well as around me, compelled me to watch it. I followed through with what I internally knew to be the right thing to do. Lo and behold, I came to know of another soul who had a somewhat similar experience to my own.

Anita's smooth, calm voice flowed to all of Lilou's questions. Then, a single statement Anita made a short way into the interview brought me to a personal moment of total truth. Anita stated that she was given a choice during her NDE to return or stay, with no judgment passed either way, just as I had been. A heart warming jolt shot straight through my core and all the doubt I'd been wrestling with, went running over the hills for good. At that moment, I knew that I just might not be crazy after all, also sensing that I had to meet her and at some point I would.

Spring, summer and fall had come and gone and in early November, winter began to settle in once again. One morning while sifting through numerous emails, I came across one sent to me by HayHouse. It was an invitation to a conference of authors in Toronto for the weekend of March 15th and 16th. Re-

reading the email several times, I realized Anita Moorjani was one of the authors scheduled to be at the conference. In a flash, I took in the full scope of it all. Anita resides on the other side of the world from me in Hong Kong, and for two days she was going to be only an hour's drive away. Knowing and trusting what I had learned, I ordered up a ticket. I felt being there would place me in Anita's path, providing a chance to meet her and fulfill a soul's desire to know of another's existence.

One of the quotes I created and use often is, "When you walk in and with love, the magic a day holds shall unfold before you." That entire weekend in March of 2014 was filled from moment to moment with a continual, crackling flow of magic. From the moment I pulled into the parking lot near the venue, I felt a bubble form around me. After turning off the SUV's engine, I sat for a few moments to stretch out from within, so as to come to totally understand this bubble. Strolling across the parking lot to the attendant's office, my attention was drawn to a beautiful young woman I assumed to be from the Islands. As I came to stand just a few feet behind the woman, her accent confirmed my assumption.

The static crackling of the magic began to rise, as she now stood within the bubble. The attendant had informed her of the fee for the full day of parking. Immediately and inexplicably, I felt all of her inner emotions. I knew the feelings to be hers as my heart sank because I could not afford the thirty dollar fee. I had several hundred dollars in my pocket, so they certainly were not my own thoughts and feelings. I also got the impression that this day was a last-resort measure to change my life.

As she desperately fished through her purse, I stepped around the woman to hand the attendant the thirty dollars, saying that it was for her. She cried out "Don't do that!" Placing my left hand on her shoulder I said "It is okay...it's okay. Wear a smile and your day will become magical." She stepped out of the bubble as I turned to pay for my parking and my gaze was met by a smiling attendant, who dropped my fee to twenty bucks.

When I turned back around to finish speaking with her, she had disappeared. I am not quite sure how, because the line of sight distance was a fair bit. Moreover, the woman would have been hard to miss, as everyone else present had on dark winter colors, while the woman was wearing a bright red coat and outfit. I am unsure as to what transpired for her, but feel she had a better chance to accomplish her life-changing objective on that day - and that was just the beginning.

Anita Moorjani was the second speaker that morning. I sat listening intently to the soft words of her experience and of her own lessons learned. During Anita's book signing I finally arrived at a moment I saw many months before, and the chance to meet her. Feeling the connection of experience with her was another magical moment, yet as I handed her my story (which is now chapter one) there was nothing. The static bubble started to fade. Undaunted, I proceeded through the day.

What I had originally thought I was there to do came and went without any significant turning point coming to fruition. It wasn't until a while later I realized I was, perhaps, getting in my own way by not allowing events to transpire. I changed into more comfortable clothes, scooping up the last copy of my story and headed downstairs from the 13th floor of the hotel for a bite to eat. In the elevator, the days events floated through my mind as I noticed the bubble form around me once again. As the elevator came to a slow, soft stop a bubbling surge within forced me to smile.

Making my way across the huge lobby, heading to the hotel restaurant, I noticed Robert Holden, another Hay House author, just slipping into an elevator. I quickened my step, thrusting the copy of my story I had in hand through the closing elevator doors. He thanked me and I thanked him as the doors came to rest together. A shiny image of myself glistened back at me from the surface of the doors. Everything underwent an extreme shift as a new path began. Off to dinner I went, just around the corner from the elevators. The magic continued to unfold as someone out of the blue paid for my dinner. Thinking back to the morning's events in the parking lot I glowed from within.

A few hours later, while back in my InterContinental Hotel room, I sat down to relax and do a bit of writing - more connecting of the dots once again, but in simple form. After six pages of individual-point-form lines, I realized I was tired and crawled into bed some time after midnight for some needed rest.

I awoke at 3:40 am to a familiar, strong, loving presence. I was immediately wide awake as I slowly slid from the bed. Walking over to the full window, I peered out and down to the base of the CN Tower, then up to its top. Bright purple lights the full length of the tower illuminated the cold night. Looking out over the city lights of Toronto's south end, I knew that today was the day I came for, yet didn't know how or why. From all I had learned up to that moment, I knew not to ask, only to follow through, allowing what would to happen.

While standing in line waiting for the doors to the auditorium to open, a woman walked up to stand behind me. As always I knew enough to spend the coins from my palm wisely, not allowing the time to go to waste. While waiting we had a pleasant conversation as I told her of my story but had no copies left to give her one. Finally the doors opened and as we walked in, she called out to a friend already inside to grab another seat for me. Her friend immediately launched her coat into a seat in the fourth row from the stage, just behind her. As I came to sit in that seat, I noticed just behind me the couple from New York City whom I sat with the day before. The bubble began to grow once again.

Doreen Virtue was one of the speakers on that Sunday morning. I knew little of Doreen and her work with angels. I had however listened to her many years before on a internet radio program, but never seriously followed her work. There was an extreme, specific magic that enveloped me, which had a considerably different feel to it than the bubble the day before, so I listened intently from within myself as she spoke. Doreen had seemingly been looking in my general direction for some time while sitting on a tall white chair up on stage. My chest started to burn from the inside out. I knew it wasn't another heart attack or anything like it, but then, suddenly, my right hand slowly went up. I actually pushed it down with my left hand, but it was too late. As I looked back to the stage, Doreen was motioning for me to stand up.

While standing up, I figured I'd simply tell my story in brief then sit back down. The words I spoke flowed as I told of the events of my death and my choice to return. An audience of around three thousand people roared into applause and cheering. Rather stunned and somewhat shocked at the response I looked around, wondering what I was going to do now! During Doreen's book signing I got to spend some time with her and Micheal out in the lobby area. I finally understood I loved the two of them, yet it only took that moment on that day to realize that I always had.

My empathic nature stood front and center most of the day as so many people wanted to meet, talk and ask questions. The bubble never really faded throughout the day, but did intensify at times. One significant instance happened while I was talking with a group of six or seven people. I noticed a woman, perhaps in her late sixties, standing quietly just behind the group. As the group slowly dispersed, she took a single step forward without saying a word. Her eyes never left mine, nor mine hers. I took a half step towards her, closing the distance a bit more. Standing still, peaceful and open, I wanted to allow her to do as she must. She stepped towards me placing her cheek on my chest and began to cry.

Wrapping my arms around her I felt all of her emotions. After a few moments, she pulled back a little and said "My husband passed away nineteen years ago and my life has been

@#&*!% up ever since." I really have to say those were the very last words I thought I would have heard come from this tiny, older woman. Her husband stood beside us, just out of sync and phase with this reality. I told her he was fine and that she should go paint and enjoy life as she once had. She asked me how I knew. At first I wasn't sure what she meant, so all I could do was give her a simple shoulder shrug. She went on to explain that she threw all of her brushes and paints away the day after her husband died.

With a big smile she gave me a final hug and thanked me before walking away. Once again, I really have no idea what became of her, though felt a sense that things were going to be better for her.

Now, as I approach my fifth new-birthday (anniversary of my NDE) two key factors have arisen in my life. The first key factor I recently came face-to-face with, was a boulder sitting on that psychological wooden skid that each of us pulls. There was a situation I tried to deal with from the start, a few days after getting out of the hospital.

An appointment had been made by the attending physician with my family doctor to discuss the biological aspects of the heart attack and its after-effects. Upon entering his office, there was little small talk other than him saying it was good to see me in his office rather than on his table, as he was also the regional coroner. As he sat down and flipped open my file, I mentioned my desire to talk with someone in regard to being out of sync and feeling like I didn't belong here. He replied that what happened was of a biological nature, so we needed to look after that first and foremost. The issue was quickly swept under the carpet and only significantly mentioned once again, though fruitlessly, at a later date.

I went about my life, starting to help people while piecing together the complex and intricate puzzle on my own. I was always aware of the desire and need to talk about it, though it never seemed to be anything more than a distant light in the darkness. It was, however, about to finally catch up to me.

Although I was unaware of it, Anita Moorjani for a second time in less than a year was going to be just an hours' drive from me. She was going to be doing a full day workshop, only this time it was South of where I live.

One morning, as I settled in to get caught up on emails and the Internet, I wasn't prepared for what was about to happen. While updating things on Facebook, I came across a simple picture of two tickets. The tickets were numbers 1 and 2. Now, at that point, I was totally oblivious to Anita returning to this area. Just the sight of those tickets, though, sent the dominoes tumbling.

In a cascading effect with several individuals involved, I came across a trailer for a documentary called *Near Death After-Effects* by Robert Neal Marshall and Yvonne Sneeden. It's a documentary about what NDE'ers go through after their experience. In watching the documentary trailer, that psychological boulder I mentioned earlier came rolling off the skid right onto me.

I wasn't expecting such a fall out, as for the most part I am and have been fine. All it took were a few words and statements by those being interviewed in the documentary and I cracked wide open like a dropped egg. For the ensuing forty-five minutes after, my internal core liquified that boulder, pushing it up and out through my eyes in a bit more liquid form. Within a few hours, I felt incredibly fantastic and just as light as I had been shortly after my NDE five years earlier.

The second key factor was a deep internal realization of the near-winning lottery ticket odds I've over come. A recent university of Michigan study shows that the chance of surviving just an average, run-of-the-mill heart attack is only 7.6%. That's 1 in 13 odds, folks; now there's a deep, dark, abysmally low factor for you to digest. Keep in mind that those stats refer to out-of-hospital attacks.

An even more significant and staggering statistic is the percentage of all heart attack survivors who see their five year mark, post heart attack. Of those who managed to stroll away from those odds against them with the initial heart attack, (don't quote me, but if I remember correctly from the global study I was entered into) 87% do not see their fifth re-birthday / anniversary. That means that only thirteen out of one hundred continue to walk life's journey as of the fifth year.

Hummm... 1/8th of 7.6 %. Now, with my left hand in front of me, palm facing me with fingers loosely spread, calculating the odds on those finger tips with my right index finger, I feel a deeply grateful sense of purpose in Being. That sense of purpose reaffirmed my understanding that we are not what we have learned to perceive ourselves to be. Although I have known this since that fateful day of February 26th 2010, situations along the way have brightened and made the fact even bigger.

If we come to understand that physical existence and life are like school, we would realize that each of us is on the verge of being kicked out as so few are learning. On the other hand, there is no judgment passed, hence we continue to bang our heads against the wall, trying to make do with no instruction manual. The teachers are there, but first you must learn to feel from within. Then and only then will you hear well enough to become aware. Then the slow process of understanding begins.

You are what everything is. Your thoughts, feelings and emotional roller coaster ride betray the you that you truly are within. You, just like everyone else throughout history, were not born with an owner's manual or hand guide. The time is upon us to come to "understand *what* we are, first and foremost, which will bring us face to face with *who* we are." With these two essential components in their proper order, this furthers all you can do as well as the "how to do". The governing factor to all things within the physical universe is the electricity of electrons (personal frequency, vibration, magnetic fields etc. etc.). The one and only true balancing emotional factor, however, is love. Love must be felt and known throughout all that you are, which brings us back to the beginning:" You are what everything is."

My stretch in time became a factor of my task. My task? A simple one: to help people, however I could, whenever I could.

What was not so simple at the time was knowing how to get to those who needed the help. I have met so many people and more every day who are or have become stuck in the quicksand of life or immobilized by the loss of a loved one, unable to live life as it originally was meant.

I can't say it's been an easy ride since that fateful day my reset button was pushed. - and pushed hard, yet when I think of all the people I've worked with and helped, it's been worth the coins from my palm to let you know of the journey and to bring this book to you.

For myself, though perhaps not easy, post-experience life has been such an amazing journey and so far removed from what any person could say was normal. The experience and process of my NDE journey allowed me to pass through the wall of the grain-of-sand perception we currently have, to step out and walk upon the beach of all that there truly is. I have learned not only to see but also to understand the vastness of sand on a beach with no visual ends.

It isn't so much that you have to dive into each grain to comprehend each one, yet by being free from the one you know of them all. This echo's the statement made to me by the Beings of 111. "The atom before you is as all others are."

In closing, I want to mention another individual I remember speaking with at the March 2014 conference in Toronto. I was heading rather quickly down some stairs to a washroom as a young man passed me on his way back up. He glanced at me as he passed and as I turned to go down the last set of stairs, he yelled out, "Hey it's you... The dead guy!" With a smile, I stopped and said "Ya, I guess so." He asked me what he needed to do with his life to be successful. "I am not a physic in the sense you think." I replied. He said, "I know, but I've been stuck lately!" I stepped back up a few stairs, placing my hand to his chest, as I felt the problem. Looking up I told him to stop getting in his own way. With a smile he further asked what I had learned from and since my experience. At the time, I could not answer him, at least not with any comprehendable short answer. In an unconscious response, however, I said, "I can show and you can choose to do."

CHAPTER 3

My Point to Begin

*"Peacefulness resides where
you choose to allow it"*

—Alan R. Stevenson

Lana wrote to me to say;

"There is often something of a turning point like this in our lives, isn't there? Thanks for sharing your story. Mine in a nutshell: I was on a path where I'd grown all I could within the church and with the ex. He was abusive and I had learned the lesson I needed to. Spirit told me one day that if I did not leave him, I would be dead in 4 years time. I did not need to test that to see if it would come true. I had grown to total trust of what I heard from Spirit which has been proven to be right each time. I now have grown past what I knew then and have a wonderful new husband."

Later on in the day of February 26th 2010, I stepped through a foggy mist with my eyelids flickering a bit, as I became consciously aware of a nurse coming through the doorway of my ICU room. She approached, at what seemed to be half speed. As she came within six or so feet from me, I felt as though two balloons were coming together. Then, there was a slight pop, for lack of a better term, that was more of a sensation rather than a sound. My groggy feeling was replaced with a completely warm, glad sensation that washed over all that I am. I felt and knew, however odd it may seem, that the nurse was rather happy to see me waking up. My previous recollection had been fading out on an OR table earlier that morning.

My new life had begun with a noticeable, extreme alteration of physical perception. As I lay in the bed of the large room, I became very aware of continual, though faint objects moving around and darting by, out at the edge of my vision. It was as though once they came to a certain point within my vision, they would disappear. This reminded me so much of the initial appearance by the Beings of 111, a smile from deep within grew on my face. I couldn't have stopped it if I wanted to.

Feeling a strong need, I got up out of bed under my own steam to wander the oval shaped ICU floor. Wearing nothing more than my gaping gown, I walked around reflecting, on the days events and analyzing to separate and sort through the surreal nature of them. The process of piecing the puzzle together had begun.

Over the coming days, weeks and even the proceeding few years, I came to fully understand a specific lesson the Beings of 111 taught me. Among the holographic images, a large chalkboard came up with dots spread out over its surface. Lines were then drawn in, connecting them all. I understood this to be a representation of life's journey. The lines between quickly faded and the dots assembled in a line touching and connected to each other.

These dots represented significant turning points along the path of our life's journey, wherein the lines connecting each one in sequence, represented how we arrived at a given point or situation. The journey between becomes a factor of our mental, emotional and physical being. Each consecutively added dot alters the overall summary of our life's story. I was also made aware of the macro-cosmic scale of the dots, as they each represent lifetimes as well. The importance of each dot added becomes relevant to the preceding ones, in that without each one, none would be possible.

It's important to understand for physical reference that this entire lesson took place in about a nanosecond. With my first point of waking up now behind me, the next was only a few short days away and every bit as significant.

As noon approached on the day following my heart attack, I was transported back to St. Catharines General Hospital. I spent a further week or so in an open ward of roughly ten beds, to begin the recuperation period from the biological trauma my body had suffered. After a few days of reorienting myself to physical life once again, I figured my feet were under me well enough to see some people. After family members visited I decided to call a woman I had started dating a couple of months before. The conversation that ensued became a very significant turning point to this moment here, right now.

I hadn't talked with Lisa in several days, and once she realized who I was, I felt her emotional state drastically change, right through the phone. Lisa's significance is that she was present the night my brother and I had the argument, just prior to the heart attack. Even with the emotional jolt I got, I went on to explain what happened, and asked if she wanted to come see me in the hospital. Sounding considerably less than enthusiastic that I'd called her, she proceeded to end the blossoming relationship in a very direct manner, then and there. Slowly reaching over to the bedside table I hung up the phone.

Moments like these, for most, are ones of great emotional and physical discernment, whereas for myself, it really became nothing. I wasn't in shock, nor was I mad, and I didn't even feel sad about what just took place. Don't get me wrong; Lisa was very important in having renewed a youthful viewpoint of passion and of the love two can share. I had, until then, spent the previous fifteen months pretty much on my own.

Although that moment seemed insignificant at the time, it was in actuality extremely important. If I was to erase several events that occurred over the previous week from my personal blackboard, how very different my life would be today! Everything that has taken place since her statements and me hanging up, simply wouldn't have happened. Learning to recognize those moments for what they truly are, as they happen, is ever so important.

Initially, I started writing down what happened to me only for my daughters to have at a later date. It wasn't until some time in April or May of 2011 I even considered the idea of writing an actual book. During work one day, Andrew, a twenty-something co-worker asked me several questions in regard to a young woman he was interested in. Andrew and I worked together in a very small area between two CNC machines, for twelve hours a day. Over several months, Andrew became the son I never had, and with me being me, I knew he was out of sorts even before he asked. He'd been seeing her to some extent, yet couldn't get the relationship to move forward, and couldn't figure out why. During that work shift I laid out pretty much all I'd learned. When I was done, his response was, "You gotta' put this sh* in a book." I laughed, saying I didn't think so, but odder things have happened to me! The toying with the idea began.

In searching for a way to convey my experience and the lessons taught by the Beings of 111, several difficulties arose. The first was during the summer of 2013, when my youngest daughter, Danika, came to stay with me for a few weeks. The two of us share a bond very similar to that of my father and I. A relationship I have cherished my entire life.

A few days prior to Danika coming to stay, I finished what I had hoped was a final rewrite of what is now chapter one. Danika has always shown an extreme intellectual level and a love of reading, so I wanted her to read what I had finished. It was in the following moments I was to come face-to-face with a dire fact I'd been unaware of since my heart attack.

Danika was sitting at the kitchen table as I slid the stapled sheets in front of her and in a nonchalant manner she agreed to read through the story. I wanted Dani to take her time and even gave her a pencil to mark it up as she saw fit. Not wanting to hover over her while she read, I headed out to the garden.

I puttered around in the garden for a bit and then sat on a garden bench that sits under a large silver maple tree. One moment I was fine, peacefully soaking up the radiating beauty of the garden and the day, and the very next I wasn't. All of a sudden I was struck with an overwhelming sadness. I could feel a specific signature to this intruding sensation and knew it didn't belong to me. Since the bench and tree are located at the end of the property, I quickly spun around looking for someone fairly close by, due to the strength of the sensation. There are several other properties that adjoin ours, so in a bit of a frantic manner, it was there I initially started looking. Suddenly and very clearly I saw Danika in my mind and took off running for the house with the internal feeling growing stronger. Bounding in one stride from the ground to the back door landing, I grabbed the outer door handle, swinging it open with a good, healthy fling.

The back door entry into the house is just off the kitchen, where Danika sat sobbing uncontrollably. With a few quick steps I covered the distance to lift her up in my arms to hug and hold onto her, allowing her to let it out. Knowing she was physically fine, and outside of saying that it's okay over and over, I didn't push her to tell me what was wrong. Looking down at the sheets on the table, I noticed only a few flipped over, so it didn't take me too long to connect the dots of the situation. But my first assumption proved to be wrong. I'd assumed she was upset by reading what I went through that day of the heart attack.

Once Danika calmed down considerably, I asked her in a soft, loving voice if that was the reason. She pulled back a bit, looking up at me and began trying to speak through her tears, saying "No, no that wasn't it at all." Reading the story and being drawn into it had been the catalyst to start her own personal moments of that day flashing back to her. Once Dani could, she explained that she had been inadvertently left for ten or so minutes that day, with the feeling and belief that I had died and was gone. The sadness I felt forced me to try and wrap her tighter in my arms so as to pull her in closer to my core, though to no avail. I tried my best to apologize for the disconnected manner in which I handled the whole situation, saying I never knew, as no one ever told me. Sitting back down, Danika being the trooper she is insisted it was alright, and she would be okay.

As I slowly sat, I felt for the first time my own heart sink into my shoe. Looking at Danika I said, "Perhaps I'm just not the right one to do this task." Reaching over in front of her to draw the sheets of paper back towards myself, she dropped a firm hand on top of them, saying she was going to finish it. Danika continued on to say that there was no one else or anyone better to tell the story, or to help the people who need it. During the conversation that ensued, she said I had to finish it and that she really wanted me to.

For me, that day was one of those hard left or right turns on the Etch-a-Sketch board of life. The strength and definitive impression on that day changed my own perception. I knew its signature didn't belong to me, nor was it generated by my own thoughts or feelings. Sure, I had had smaller situations almost daily since the heart attack, yet never as powerful or as impacting. This became my personal point to begin and a greater realization that perception must be the starting point.

CHAPTER 4

Your Point to Begin

*"Proof life is boot camp is in
how many times it has kicked you"*

—*Alan R. Stevenson*

Samantha wrote to me to say;

"I do have to say, the things you taught me about energy, how it attracts, and how you can protect yourself, really really helped me. I was on a total dead track and desperate to get rid of the pain. Many thanks once again."

With little direction or know-how, I went back to work contemplating putting a book together. I had a few people I knew read some of the writing I had done. I tried writing from different perspectives, yet time and time again the feedback responses were considerably less than impressive. Blank stares and slight shoulder shrugs with little to no eye contact made it fairly easy to connect the dots. I was repeatedly told I'd have to come back to earth or at least down out of the clouds, to make it more understandable. In early 2014 I scrapped the rough draft and ideas I originally started with.

During the summer of 2014, I took a day long trip on my motorcycle to visit with my father. This trip was to spend some of those coins from my palm with a human being I love dearly and respect above all others. The bike ride in the freedom of the sun and wind was but a much-needed perk. After a nearly three hour ride, I met my father and stepmother at their house, located in a blink of a town called Bervie. A little while after arriving we headed into the lakeside town of Kincardine for lunch. I rode the bike into town as it needed gas after the long ride there, while Dad and Lynn took their convertible.

It was good to see them both, as always, and no mention of the book came up during lunch, which was my original intent all along. This day was all about some needed father and son time.

The relationship my father and I have has always been based on a deep respect and love. During my younger years, I often referred to him as my best friend. For the vast majority of my childhood years, the two of us were together often. For most of my life, I never truly understood that so few men have this relationship with their fathers. However time has a way of changing things we do not want changed. Over the last fifteen or so years, the two of us have become somewhat estranged. Contact and expression of that love and respect is and always will be there, though not as often. I am always mindful of the fact that the person I've become was originally shaped and molded foundationally by my father. For that, I am forever grateful.

After lunch, we headed back to the house, only to turn around again and head back out a short while later. The area is very wide open countryside, where even your neighbor's house is a long distance phone call. Out there, you just don't plan any short trips. Dad was driving Lynn over to Port Elgin, another lakeside tourist town, roughly thirty miles further North of Kincardine. I have a great number of fond memories of Port Elgin from the summer I spent there when I was fifteen. Anyway, Dad and I planned to meet up at the ice cream parlor near the marina in Port to have an ice cream and walk the pier. It had been nearly thirty years since the last time the two of us were there.

Dad was cutting across country on some back roads that weren't suited for the bike, so I headed along Hwy #21 that runs between Kincardine and Port Elgin. The landscape along there was once farmland on both sides of the roadway. Now, however, it's densely populated with huge, white wind turbines. It was a warm, sunny day and one of a sparse few that summer, becoming lost in the freedom of the ride. Midway through the ride, my rule of no thinking about the manuscript for the day was broken. My thoughts redirected to the situation of how to change the contents to make it more understandable, or whether I even should.

Roaring along the highway with a smile on my face, I suddenly could no longer hear the throaty sound of the bike, not even the wind rushing past my ears. A deep, peaceful silence grew from within, numbing most of my external senses, as an interesting concept came to mind: If I am to show you the other side (as so many refer to it), and the lessons from there, should I step across and use physical reality concepts to illustrate it?

The problem with that is, by using such a framework, the minuscule physical shell is reaffirmed, cementing you here in the physical. Though you may not think so, this doesn't allow you to step out upon that beach of endless sand. Only by means of a strong shift in perception may we come to understand that all of the physical "here" originates from the other side. So it is that I'm to put a hand through the wall of our current, grain-of-sand perception to try and pull you through. Meanwhile, always keep in mind my main statement, *"I am nothing more than that which you already are."*

While considering the best point from which to start, I came to realize the dawn of time was where we, as a whole, chose the path and direction of our current perception. Thousands of years ago, we as a species and race of intelligent beings, had a choice in how to perceive ourselves and the physical world around us. After coming out of a long period of learning basic survival skills, we garnered enough intelligence to begin to ask the "whys" about ourselves and those of the physical reality that we exist in. With that intelligence, we started to become more aware of some simple facts about the physical world, by way of our five senses, as well as the fact that we had these senses to begin with.

Although there are many modes to perception itself, for simplification purposes I am going to use a *"down the road to your left"*, and a *"down the road to your right"* scenario. Keep in mind that this is simply an illustrative story to paint a bit of a comical picture of our beginnings.

Imagine a group - mind you a very large group - consisting of pretty much the entire human race. They're standing at the edge of the roadway or path to perceiving their external world. They look left, then look right, contemplating which way to go. They asked themselves as well as each other, "Which way is the right way?" At that point of our perceptive development, a choice was made whether to turn left or right, so to speak.

Initially, a few brave souls stepped out to the left and started to walk down that path. The majority of the people still standing there looked at one another and with a bit of a shrug, started to follow them. I have come to feel that it was probably more like the majority stepped to the left, while a few true brave souls decided to do something completely different then the masses, and headed down the path less traveled, to the right. *Now remember, this is about perception and the mass concept to perceive our physical reality.*

At a point in our history the "left" group called out to the travelers who went off to the right, "Hey you're going the wrong way... it's this way! Come look, we can prove it!"

The majority from the group on the right stopped and turned, then walked back towards the group that originally went left. The remaining travelers on the right, though few, continued onward. As the wandering group approached, the individual who did all the initial yelling stepped forth. He bent over, without uttering a single word and picked up a stick, thick as your arm. Tapping it a few times in his opposite hand, he proceeded to ding an absent-minded Charlie, standing next to him, right on the noggin, and down went Charlie.

Clad in his fur and animal skin clothing, this somewhat self-appointed leader then continued to facilitate on and on just about the mere stick. Stating the stick is more compact, making it harder than Charlie's head. He continued on saying that once Charlie had been hit on the head, a bunch of domino kinda things inside Charlie toppled over, hence he fell to the ground. Why he fell rather than floated upwards or even just floating in mid air is, however an entirely different question.

He went on to say that the ground Charlie landed on was also much harder than Charlie was, so it stopped him from going any further downward. With a fairly vague look upon his face and scratching his head he said, "On top of it all, there is a mystical property thingy going on with the ground. I'm not quite sure what that is right at the moment, but, I will figure it out." The crowd's eyes widened, and jaws dropped open to a rounded position, their hands clutched in front of them saying, OHHH so that's why! And if I'm not mistaken, I believe the word "sheeple" was invented later that afternoon.

I apologize for the injection of a bit of humor, but I felt I had to, to try and simplify things, due to some advice given by my father. During a phone conversation in early 2015, he told me he felt I would scare the bejesus out of far too many people with the account of my heart attack, not to mention the physical, human process of dying. Even after I told him the book would have little to do with heart attacks other than to mention some significant signs to watch for, and a few recommendations, he still reiterated his statement.

I knew dad was trying hard to make a point as he brought several valid factors up. He reminded me of his above average IQ at a point in his life, then added that he's been an avid reader most of his life, and at that even he had a hard time understanding what I wrote. He did however come to understand it, but only after re-reading the piece several times. He went on to say that many readers may end up having far too hard a time with it. In the end, they might never finish reading the book. All in all, it brought to light the potential to do a huge disservice to them, the readers and, ultimately, an even bigger one to myself.

I did my best to make a point that I had to get people to drastically open their minds and change their current perspective, just as he had done until he came to understand it.

That afternoon we discussed it at length, mentioning I'd recently watched a documentary called "Particle Fever". During portions of the documentary, some physicists of CERN filled huge blackboards with very large equations. I used this to illustrate the fact that I understood the dilemma. What looks extremely complicated to just about everybody else is a piece of cake to the physicists, who use those equations in their work, day in and day out. After painting a clear picture for my dad, I said I was feeling myself to be in somewhat of the same predicament. His tone changed as he said I would find a way.

After saying good-bye and putting in place the love I felt as I always do at the end of our talks, I slowly hung up the phone. Standing there for a few brief moments with my hand still on the receiver, as it hung on the wall, I gently rested my forehead to my forearm, once again feeling the enormity of the daunting task.

While resting that way, a memory of lying in the hospital to recuperate flashed through my mind. I recalled a day where I was a bit over-whelmed by the task as an art-deco style cartoon played out, where a 250,000 piece puzzle was dumped and spread all over a huge gymnasium floor. Standing in the middle of it all, I was going to have to put the puzzle together.

Later on that same night, I walked about outside to ponder Dad's heart-felt advice. Though it was a mighty bit cold, I gathered up the Being that I am, doing my best to relive the moments in which Tiger and the three Beings outlined this task. Though the task was outlined by them, it was left to me to find a way to implement what they had shown me. Then, just as it often happens, it clicked! A few weeks prior to that evening, I had sat right here as I placed pen to paper awaiting what was to come through, as I sometimes do.

Now after dumping once again the content of the book, I feel that I perhaps have a better grasp of how it should be. I knew originally it would be a difficult undertaking at best. I mean, how do you tell people about a place they have not been, or at least can't remember, for good reasons? How do you begin to tell them about a different way in which to perceive themselves and all that is around them. How do you explain that achieving all they wish to do, have and be is a simple, natural process and that the current mode of near-total unconscious perception of their everyday lives and doings is skewed by that original choice to wander down the road to the left long ago.

For prosperity's sake, I shall draw a bit more of an analogy to further the concept. Most of us have known a close friend or family member who went off to a tropical island or foreign land we've never been to. When they returned, you more than likely asked what it was like. They proceeded to tell you about it with joy and excitement, describing scenes and different moments of the trip. You, yourself probably tried to follow along by piecing together the imagery from the framework and parameters of your own past experiences.

It is here that the translation falls apart and far short. The pieces of the puzzle you are using are yours and have little to do with that specific place. Your puzzle pieces have a different look, fitment and feel to them. Your past experiences allowed you, at least, a remote idea of how to perceive the place where your friend or family member had been. Still, the integral part that we cannot help but step over is the most important one. Only the person who did the traveling knows of and holds the essence of having been there. That's a problem in this situation that, unfortunately, cannot be overcome.

Earlier, I showed you what I had, in previous attempts, dryly outlined by telling you about the beginnings of science, math, and physics in a round-about, comical way. I also stopped with the story line on purpose, because I needed you to stop and change up your thoughts and start to let go, if even just a little bit for now.

To understand, you must let go of the way in which you think and feel about things. You must start to reach out with what you are within. *Who* you are at this very moment is the sum total of all your thoughts and feelings of all your experiences, yet it still is not *what* you are. Perhaps, in time, you'll choose to stop along the edge of your own path or roadway and look back over your shoulder just long enough to hear within yourself "Maybe...just maybe..."

What was on that piece of paper I wrote upon? Now as it sits here in front of me once again, I feel with all that I am, just as I did when I wrote it. *"I want to show you... I really want to show you the other side and all that I have learned from all that I was shown."*

I want to do this, not so you can go through my death to experience it for yourself, for that is not important and *"It does not matter."* Trust me when I say you will have one of your own at some point. It is my sincerest wish that by reading this book in its entirety, your perception of your day to come will change from one of fear, to a clear understanding. With that understanding, you will be able to live the life you were always meant to live.

We feel far too many fears today about life, death and the aspects of living, due to our inability to perceive life and death for what they actually are. Fear has created a fair-sized gap in our understanding and our ability to perceive well enough to move forward. That little, four-letter word is the most common one I hear from the people I've worked with. We are slowly regressing back to a point in time where nearly everything that moved created fears within us.

Our current level of global societal development has been driven by that internal yearning to know, to truly understand what we are, once and for all. Unfortunately, our current state of development and the perception of where we believe ourselves to be are two very different and distant points. If gauged against our actual inner potential, we are currently little more than toddlers in a crowded daycare.

Our interaction with one another is rudimentary at best and strained to its fringe points by our need to be overly defensive. That defensiveness, mind you, has been taught and slowly learned over the last century or so. If perhaps you stop for a moment to see, realize and feel the difference between those toddlers and the adults in the room with them, a macro cosmic-scale effect should come into play. In this scenario, the early childhood caretakers become our teachers and guides.

It is possible you may think and/or feel some of the statements I've made to be a bit harsh. The fact is, if you had witnessed the potential future for the human race and this planet, a few harsh statements would be acceptable. It is a future I do not talk about or even think of for good reasons. I don't talk about it for the same reason that components of a neutron bomb are not brought together in a single area, due to the potential of one being assembled. Once you come to understand how we actually create our personal moments to come, I am sure you will forgive me.

I stay fairly well rooted in the current moment, only stretching out to the next few to follow. This is a lesson I've learned and then implemented into my life what I was shown.

Your personal point to begin must be your perception of yourself, for you are not what you have learned and come to believe yourself to be, nor are your physical surroundings.

CHAPTER 5

The Science of Reality

"To be an expert published author they say you need a degree. Well then... I got my Ph. D. in Life from having died, writing the thesis with my heart while I was there, then graduated due to what I'd learned."

—Alan R. Stevenson

Anna wrote in to say:

"Alan, thank you so much for sharing your story... it really helped me today. I just found out that someone I care about just died of suicide. He had been trying for a while.... simply choosing to let go and reading your story made it bearable by knowing that he was tired, he just could not continue to fight with the illusions, he needed to return to a peaceful existence and made the choice to go! I rejoice in your choice to stay and to guide us to a more meaningful purposeful existence.

Choosing to Be!.... no matter how hard it is....."

We exist in a physical world that often makes little sense, yet in that simple fact an illusion was created long ago, then passed down through the ages. After getting through a period in our history where the Gods were responsible for nearly everything that happened, a loosely based *cause and effect* understanding of our physical world was adopted. This process started to use a bit of logical reasoning to explain the things that happened. Beliefs about our existence became more concrete, as there were those who went about sorting out the physical world by pointing out simple and obvious facts at first. The process allowed those who lived in fear of all that moved or made noise to better understand their surroundings. The concept stayed in place for over a millennium. Then, another method slowly stepped to the forefront for acceptance to understand and answer new questions that arose from our existence.

Science became the way in which we breathed a little easier at night about the things we, as a whole, didn't understand and the initial process of common sense couldn't explain. The old, original belief systems of long ago gave way to clearer understanding through new findings, due largely in part to the work of science. The process itself appealed to our common sense, which was the backbone of what carried us through up to that point.

It is not very difficult to come to a few simple common sense conclusions after witnessing a hammer strike a piece of metal. Within that example, the principle of the physicality of our surroundings using common sense becomes a little too obvious. From a scientific point of view, however, the hammer has force applied to it, creating physical movement, gaining momentum until the hammer meets resistance from an opposing physical object or loses its driving force. The hammer in this case struck another piece of metal, creating a bang, along with a short duration of ringing.

Science structured itself around that common sense and began to evolve with its acceptance growing over the next few hundred years. Many new, brilliant and curious-minded individuals wanting to be scientists were attracted to the concept and process. By this time, the framework of scientific methodology, scientific experimentation, leading to scientific proof was set. Science grew in leaps and bounds with some of the most profound findings in human history over the last hundred and fifty years.

With these new understandings, our perception of many things changed from what it was just a mere fifty years ago. That evolving change in perception becomes a quantum leap if you compare a cave dweller of ten thousand years ago to modern man. On the other side of the coin, though, what we understand today won't even scratch the surface of fifty years from now. However, I wonder if the understanding we will possess fifty years from now will be due to breakthroughs in science or just a huge leap of understanding in human consciousness and the abilities of that consciousness.

Prior to the turn of the twentieth century, a few scientists began to postulate something more, unseen, but at the time not scientifically provable, nevertheless it was there in the fabric of physical space. Science advanced over the short term and then finally found the atom. This became a huge leap for science and a turning point for so many new discoveries and a clearer understanding of the world around us.

Science went about reverse engineering and disassembling physical matter down to the atom. It took reality apart, down to to its cells, molecular structure, chemical makeup, and elements, then finally to the atom. Their findings set them back on their heels when they got to the point of nothingness. The mode of linear thinking that had been created long ago hindered their ability to believe that the premise of physical matter and reality was that you start with nothing. It was a contradictory turning point to say the least, as one of science's foundations is that you can not get something from nothing! So, a new division of science known as quantum physics and mechanics was created to delve deeper into its mysteries to try and help save the day.

Science enjoyed a long duration of discovery, having made some of the most amazing discoveries over the past few centuries, where some miraculous-minded individuals stepped up to the plate and knocked it right out of the park for the home team of the Human Race. But, not so much of late. Science's arrogance to dismiss given topics by stating that something does not have any merit to warrant any study, investigation, or money invested, is slowly becoming its own undoing. The atom became the foundation on which so many new marvels of the modern world came about, or were they just tragedies of the atomic and nuclear age?

The Reality of Science

> "There are only two ways to live your life.
> One is as though nothing is a miracle.
> The other is as though everything is a miracle."
>
> —Albert Einstein

Marie wrote in to say;

"What an incredible story, Alan. I was a little nervous about reading it, though the subject of the survival of death has always fascinated me.

I am intrigued by the 6 foot tiger that spoke to you... always something new to learn. Wow. Thanks so much for sharing!"

Science, since its inception, has always been taken so very seriously as the last word on anything and everything's potential to be real. But before we proceed, I wish to point out a quote by scientist and physicist Niels Bohr, who once said: *"Everything we call real is made of things that cannot be regarded as real."*

I find it extremely odd that on one hand, science will blatantly dismiss something outright that seems rather simplistic, then expect you to buy into and accept the Big Bang, that theorizes everything currently in the known physical universe started from a pea-sized container of energy.

Since finding the atom, most of what science has done is hypothesize and theorize about the dimension from which it came as well as anything else deemed worthy and of interest to them. Science's contradiction lies in that its modes and models are all of the physical, while trying to adjust or offset those models for the fact that our physical, material reality isn't really physical at all. Science will struggle continually until they step out of the box and release the stranglehold of doctrine that leans toward the solid world view. However, the time is upon us as fresh young minds broach the gap and dogma of old with the open-minded curiosity of the new quantum physics and the willingness to proceed down the rabbit's hole.

Science was conceived at a time and in a manner I like to refer to as "Conception By Perception". It's a method wherein conception is the act of conceiving an idea or concept, then by applying a set of principles with a plan in place, the original idea is constructed. Conception also refers to the understanding of a grand design or, say, an artist's conception of a far-off newly-discovered planet. This is a mental beginning point of piecing together the idea.

Perception, as we all know, is as varied as the number of individuals perceiving, though with a few loose parameters, a standard of sorts can be created. You can have two or more people laying down in a meadow looking at clouds on a lazy, relaxing afternoon, but seldom do they see the same shape within those clouds, due to individual perception. This is where Bobby sees a dog, Suzy sees a horse, and Sandy, well... she sees a mountain range, all in the same solitary cloud in the sky.

Pieces of another puzzle

> "When you become amazed with Life...
> Amazing things begin to happen."
>
> —*Alan R. Stevenson*

Kate wrote in to say;

"Thank you Alan! As an empath I love this beautiful description of your experience. We truly are all one and all love. I have chosen to live my life to the fullest in service to myself and the world, in whatever way I choose. Namaste xxx"

What if God handed each of us an individual piece to a puzzle having over seven billion pieces , saying, "There, now go put it together"? I believe once we see and understand that to be exactly what that Being did, we shall move more in the direction originally intended.

Sometimes we have a hard time seeing the connection between the things we see, think, e-motionalize and do, because they are so very different from one another. This creates a mental and e-motional separation between given things. That doesn't necessarily mean they do not go together, only that we can't see just how some things are connected. If you think about the West and East coasts of North America for example, they are so very different from one another, right down to the people who live along each coastal landscape. Nevertheless, those land masses are connected by the land in the middle that, once again, is so very different from either coastline.

There are small groups forming from within various and very different Scientific disciplines, appearing here and there all over the world. Their focus is to connect previously dissociated concepts and ideas with one another. Science's next huge growth spurt will come by way of connecting dissociated components being studied in different areas where the connection is not obvious, yet will click into place, forming a larger piece of the whole and bigger picture.

Science needs to be utilized more for the betterment of the Human Race and not the militarized dollar. I still remember a segment during the holograms of the dimensional effects of the atomic and hydrogen bomb blasts. If you think of an old, tall tree as being the physical world blast effects, then its root system would be the dimensional blast effects.

Perhaps in time to come, sooner rather than later, multiple disciplines of science will work more closely together instead of the closed-in black box. Perhaps we will also be more open to exploring different concepts as opposed to being outright dismissive as to their having any merit worthy of study. For the Human Race to advance, science needs to be a part of the process.

CHAPTER 6

The Spark of All There Is

" It is not so much about not knowing as it is about realizing that you already know."

—Alan R. Stevenson

*C**helsie* wrote to me to say;

"Thank you Alan!! As a nursing student I have had the amazing experience of being around those that are about to die and those who have died. Many talk to people or guides and it always amazes me and feel truly honored to be with them as they make their journey and each time has been life changing for me. Thank you for sharing your story! It really helps to put things in perspective!"

As a young boy I had some truly amazing adventures, as well as my fair share of misadventures along the way. Those misadventures were truly no less amazing, but that's only because I'm sitting here now reflecting back on them. At the time, those misadventures were - shall we say, lessons that needed to be learned. Then there are those scattered, extraordinary moments mixed in amongst the adventures that are so far outside of our normal routine that they force us to stop and go, "Hmm," either from amazement, shock, or simply having been dumbstruck. Frozen in our tracks, we're compelled to give a good justifiable scratch or rub to the top of our heads. I've always found it to be somewhat peculiar that, when we're seized in the grip of these types of moments, we reach to scratch that particular spot.

For me, falling out of a car at five years old was one of those slow motion moments, though I remember one of a few years later quite vividly as a true, first time head scratching moment. Back in 1971 or early in 1972, I went to my very first NBA basketball game. We drove over the Rainbow Bridge from Fort Erie, Ontario to the Buffalo Auditorium, to see the Buffalo Braves play. I had just started playing basketball, so as you can imagine, it was one of those huge childhood adventures.

Walking into the auditorium among all the adults was like walking through a dense forest. My internal excitement was at a peak, though I was unaware that the night was going to get bigger and better as it went on. During half time, the game announcer called out the numbers from the middle of the program guide. With the program laying open across my lap, I looked on in disbelief as my numbers came to life, while the announcer called out, 1...., 7..., 3..., 5..., 0. I was so stuck in my own disbelief of what just took place my dad had to tell me to get up and head down to the floor to see what I'd won. My coach stated that if it was a half court shot he would take it.

On my way to the announcer's table, I had to walk right behind the players' bench. Bob McAdoo, Randy Smith, Bob Kauffman, Elmore Smith, to name a few, rounded out the team back then. Collecting my dinner for two prize, I turned to look up and around the auditorium. An internal sense of sheer awe came over me as I took in the immensity of the place and all the people. In the very next moment, though, I became somewhat apprehensive, thinking I might not find my way back to my seat. Prior to that night, I hadn't been to a game or event in anything bigger than a high school or university gym.

One of the seemingly foolish whims I had that night was to get some of the players' autographs. Even though everyone thought it was childish, I went prepared with one of those big, thick red pencils and a piece of line paper all folded up anyway. After the game ended and we were all making our way out, I tried to figure out how I was going to get to where the players were. That just wasn't going to happen, though, as security had something totally different in mind. Being an eight-year-old kid, I gave up rather quickly on the idea, not wanting to get too far separated or possibly lost. I decided it was best to head for the main entrance and exit area to meet up with everyone else.

Doing my best with the thick crowd, I suddenly and for no apparent reason pushed and then stumbled through to a clear opening totally void of people - all but one. For the next several moments, everything seemed to be moving in slow-motion as I looked up to see OJ Simpson striding by. He was walking across this near-perfect circular clearing, heading into the Buffalo auditorium while everyone else was leaving. He was the last person

I expected to run into that night - a night in which I went with my little boy eyes wide and glistening to see a basketball game, only to run into the number one NFL player of the time.

I wasn't much of a football fan, however I did know who he was. Reacting quickly I took off after OJ. Catching up to him, I reached out and gently tugged on the left side of his long winter coat. He turned to look down as I thrust my pencil and paper upwards, asking for his autograph. Fulfilling my request undaunted, he asked if I had enjoyed the game while handing back my paper and pencil. I couldn't remember until just now, but the Braves lost the game that night. I remember saying to OJ that it was too bad they lost, but the game was really something to see.

He turned and walked away, disappearing among all the other dark winter coats. In a bit of a daze, I stood there still as a statue, while time just wouldn't return to normal speed. Dumbstruck by the moment, I'd forgotten I was supposed to meet up with my teammates, coaches and dad at a previously specified spot. It wasn't too far away, as I could see a few of them standing there already when I turned to head in that direction. With reality slowly coming back into sync, I made my way toward them, holding up my piece of paper with a huge smile on my face and shouting, "You're never going to believe this!"

I shared the true story above to illustrate an amazing moment I experienced because there's a high probability you yourself have experienced something similar in your past. Oh sure, there are different people, different times, places, etc. in yours, yet what is common to these physical world life stories is what they create within us. It's something so familiar you can wrap your arms around it.

The vivid, sideways trip I took during my NDE is an experience few have to begin with and still fewer remember. Only a handful ever writing about it. Illustrating the story above was easy, though the same cannot be said for what is to follow shortly. The hardest part of my task now is to take you on a journey you more than likely can't remember having been on before.

The most amazing moment of my life to date was a point during my NDE, though now as I ponder that statement, it does sound a bit odd. If you think about it for a second or two, you just might have one of those head scratching sessions. I mean, let's face it, the most amazing moment of my life was during a time I was dead? I think I just might scratch my own head over that one. Nevertheless, the most amazing moment of my life was when the Beings of Three showed me the atom. To think of it with the clarity I learned to have while I was there still makes me tingle even today.

Before we begin the journey down that road, I want to bring to light several other very important lessons learned prior to the holographic edification process. Directly after Tiger's first lesson of "it does not matter", I learned something much more important, which was in regard to the conscious status level from Being to Being. I emotionally felt a need to lower my head in unbelievable awe of the Teacher. As I began to reflect that awe by diminishing my thoughts and emotional content toward my own state and status of Being, the Teacher connected, not with me, yet directly to me, to ignite an internal realization of a statement that Being then made. *"I am nothing more or less than that which you already are."* This statement was to be the foundational premise for all that was to follow and more importantly, one I now use often in my daily life.

During my sideways step to the *"other side"* of physical reality, I wasn't standing or sitting, in any typical, common sense perspective. Once I slipped from the molecular glove of my body, the physical world I knew had been removed. I was there as nothing more than the core essence of my Being. The very foundation from which we all originate provides a consciousness, that is, the ability of awareness. This is a conscious state that others who have had NDE's, mentioned, having had a feeling or sense of being everything, everywhere. I'd rather say that it's a state hard to define in physical terms, due to our physically confining and limiting parameters. The very parameters we use to define the physical reality in which we live limits us. Those limiting boundaries fall away on "the other side" and are no longer present. Our conscious awareness of those physical limiting aspects of life has always the hardest to avoid.

The common reference of *"the other side"* used today is such a huge misnomer, in that it's not to one side or the other, nor is it above or below anything. Our daily use of linear thinking created a need for us to place it somewhere so that we could better comprehend it. The fact is that it's right here all around us, within the same space you currently occupy. It isn't one step up or a step over dimensionally either, though it is within your physical reality. Not that it is undetectable as many do feel it from time to time, yet it is merely just ever so slightly invisible to our perception.

Let me explain it another way. Think of a small neon yellow glass cube for a moment. The physical, molecular structure of the glass you can see, feel and touch is a representation of the physical reality we exist in. The neon yellow color throughout the glass cube becomes a representation of where "the other side" is.

It is merely the food coloring stirred into a bowl of water. The water is never consciously aware that the food coloring is present, yet the coloring is aware of both states. We, as physical Beings, are only aware of this physical dimension, with rare exceptions. The Beings we refer to in a variety of ways, that exist only as our true essence know of and are aware of their dimension as well as ours.

You should be able to see that the physical and non-physical are mixed within one anothers' volume of space. It is only by way of our linear thinking, based on our own physical reality experiences and perception of life and death, that we're compelled to separate the two. Once you get past the internal questioning of whether it's yellow coloring and glass, to see that it's merely yellow glass, and all one, a greater importance is realized that shall become more apparent as you go forward.

In the diagram below, you can clearly see the defining differences between having an NDE and completing the journey and process on to what we refer to as Heaven. During an NDE one can proceed to a certain point. There are no defined barriers, it is simply a known point. A complete transition is a point crossed that only allows you to come back to the edge of physical reality. I later came to understand that I could not cross over to where the Beings of 111 were, or I would not have return to physical reality.

With a few lessons learned shortly after arriving on the other side, my true sense of Being started pushing through my lifelong belief system. A system of belief and perception that had been constructed during my forty-seven years of physical life began to unravel. While being there with Tiger and the Teachers, I felt an unbelievable sense of my essence of Being, which had form without any actual form. This is the state from

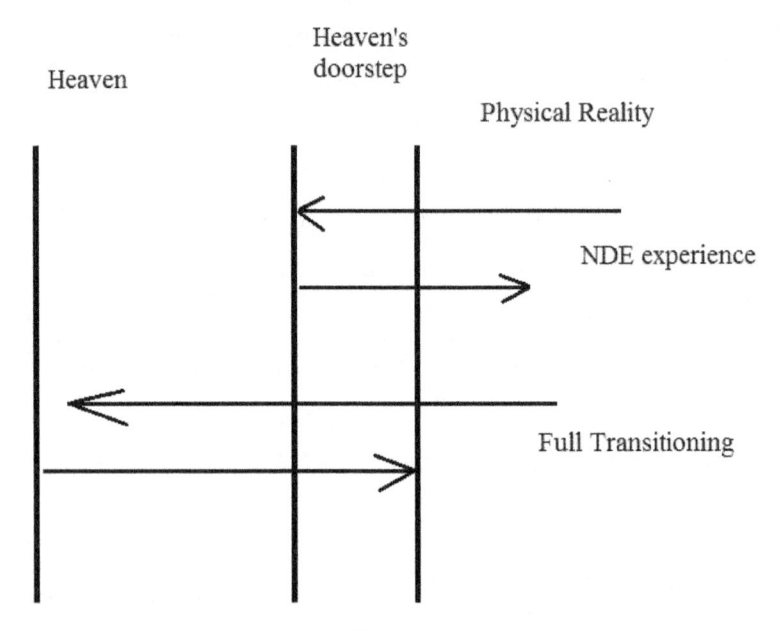

Physical acuminate of Non-physical dimensional structure

which we originate and which we return to upon physical death. This physical existence we participate in is actually the "afterlife", in that it is secondary to our primary state of Being. We are the hand, so to speak, that slips within the biological glove. An emotional response to my growing fascination with this new found state prompted a process deep within to try and perceive it all. It wasn't so much a dumbstruck moment, as it was more of a "WOW!" moment. While trying to take it all in, Tiger and the teachers came to my aid, as they initiated the holographic images.

The holograms illuminated slightly off to my right between Tiger and myself. Viewing the holograms was quite different than watching a movie per se, as I was in some way connected to them as well. The initial images were in regard to the elevating, emotional fascination I was experiencing with the true sense of my Being, hence my direct connection to the images. I was, however, about to become even more aware of that connection. At the precise moment my fascination switched to a curiosity about the holograms themselves, they, in turn changed, illustrating how I was viewing them. My connection was fully realized here by the change of what I thought, or felt, influenced to a certain degree the images themselves, though the Beings were in control at all times.

To help illustrate the holograms, I want to paint a bit of a better picture for you. An artist goes through a process prior to creating a sketch from his or her own mind. The picture they wish to draw is first and foremost created within themselves, mentally and emotionally. They see it clearly and exactly, long before going about transferring it to a physical piece of paper or canvas. By choosing specific points upon the surface in varying degrees, their original internal concept is illustrated in a 3D manner. The holograms to some degree are similar, in that specific sub-atomic particles were chosen in varying degrees, then illuminated to create the movie-like images.

Were they physical in nature? No, they were not, which defies your need to think of them in linear terms. Audible sound waves of typical communication from person to person do not have a basis in which to travel, since it would be like trying to drive a freight train on sand. Therefore it is done in an image format, where a watermelon is a watermelon and not misconstrued due to language barriers. Communication from Being to Being is done from within, yet the holograms were, for the most part, exterior to those present.

There were many times during the edification process when I just didn't have a clear enough understanding of what I was being taught. This lack of understanding created a deviating sidestep during the main focus and flow of a lesson. It was during these specific times that I became more aware of my connection to the images as they changed and continued to do so until I fully understood.

Deviating from the main focus this way wasn't unlike an information lecture or seminar you may have attended. During seminars I've attended, audience members asked questions that were then answered by the facilitator for clarification. The original flow and main focus of the instruction got back on track directly after. In simple terms, when I didn't quite understand something, it was immediately clarified with a different set of images, and then we moved on. The times when Tiger reminded me that "it does not matter" were somewhat different, having more to do with my physical reality concepts questioning the lessons being shown.

The initial focus of a lesson would resume once a thorough understanding was felt on my part at the correct deep level. The images began streaming to show and convey the extreme sense of form without perceived form I was experiencing. You may have at one time or another wondered how our physical reality could be constructed of something that is so close to being nothing? This was my point of incredible fascination that was being answered.

Once my inquisitive aspect was satisfied the images changed and continued on to illustrate a sub-sub-sub level from which nearly all things begin. It is a starting point, if you will, that builds up to the atom's existence. For use as a reference point, the *"other side"* would be up to but not including the point where atoms come together to form actual physical structure. It's at this stage that physical matter comes into being, thus creating its own dimension within the same volume of space, or the glass cube and neon yellow coloring becoming one.

I want to take a moment to outline an analogy of a physical process that will hopefully help with comprehending the most important premise of our essence of Being. Since I was a baker and chef sometime ago, I like to use the idea of baking a cake to illustrate how things are in the sub-atomic world. If, perhaps, you get a bit stuck or lost while reading through some of the really thick stuff, just keep in mind the following process. Though other analogies are outlined along the way, this one may be of help to a number of you.

Some of you may have gone through the process of baking a cake and even if you haven't, the process is fairly simple to follow. You start by gathering multiple ingredients according to a recipe on your kitchen table. You then go about combining and mixing all the dry ingredients, then the wet ingredients in separate bowls (I want you to take special notice here that the wet and dry ingredients have each transformed into something different from their original individual states.) Then you bring the contents of the two bowls together into one, and mix them till they transform again in state and appearance to a batter. After putting the batter through the process of baking, it has transformed once again. Once cooled and assembled, a further transformation takes place and then once again as it is iced and decorated.

As you sit down to eat a piece of that cake, you're not likely to think about each of the individual ingredients that went into its creation. The finished slice of cake on your dessert plate doesn't exactly resemble anything you started out with. Physical reality is much like the cake, in that it no longer resembles its initial ingredients or components. Thinking of the ingredients that went into baking the cake is not going to add any enjoyment to eating a slice, yet as we take a bite out of life, thinking about physical reality's ingredients and components are going to be more than just a little helpful.

One of the more important differences you should come to understand between physical and non-physical reality is the way in which each is formed. The point from which our true essence of Being originates is one of "from the inside out". The illustration of the cake baking process should help you to understand some important factors, such as components being combined and then transforming. This illustrates the coming together of particles and the transformational process of the non-physical becoming physical. Another form of "from the inside out" would be to watch a time-lapse film of a flower growing from bud to bloom, which is a near-perfect analogy.

Although the initial ingredients of physical reality are from the inside out, the way we do things here in our physical reality is somewhat different. Here, for the most part, we primarily add something to another physical object's exterior surface, as with the cake once it is removed from the oven. You place one layer onto another, then add on the icing, then add decorative piping and any other physical items you wish to the cake's surface. The importance of coming to fully understand this, has to do with the actual way in which we create our moments to come. This applies not so much to the longer term ones, but more so to the short term. If you think of your next few minutes of life as that blooming flower, you'll get a better sense of what I am saying and the unfolding of life becomes clearer.

Keeping in mind the cake baking process now, to illustrate how multiple sub-level components come together, then give way to the next level. This is where components of the sub-sub-sub level (all cake ingredients assembled on the table) come together, then that dimensional level gives way to the next sub-sub level, (the separate wet and dry stage) which gives way to the next sub level (mixed cake batter stage) in turn giving way to the atomic level, (baking process) which comes together to form our physical reality (decorated, finished cake). Each creates its own dimension, though it occupies the exact same volume of space. Although the same comprehension problem exists with a Russian wooden dolls analogy, whereas there is another one inside each one as you open them up, the idea, however, is exemplified.

There was a point when the holographic images came to that of an atom as a fairly large sphere in front of me. I was doing my best by this time to keep a level e-motional state, not wanting to deviate again from the main focus of what I knew to be of great importance. It was here that one Teacher stated *"The atom before you is as all others are"*. Though I came to learn quite some time later that there are actually a large variety of atoms, what was meant by the Being's statement was still understood. The statement was about the function and foundational premise of atoms.

By way of thought, Tiger instructed me to observe the most central point within the atom. Once I could feel that point within myself he further instructed me to move to that point. Understanding what Tiger meant, I immediately went to the nucleus of the atom. At first I felt a minor surge of trepidation, in thinking I might get squished among the rapidly oscillating protons and neutrons. It was fairly easy to bring my emotions back to a more balanced level once I was within the nucleus. It was kind of like being among a bunch of huge beach balls, but with no physical surface to speak of, as I flowed and intermixed with them. The oscillation or vibration so many speak of today has to do with the atom's nucleus. That oscillation is what creates the frequency also spoken of by many.

The following is an important lesson to understand, for it is the foundation of this book. Later in the book, I will be bringing all of the important aspects together for clarity.

I returned from the central point of the atom to my original spot, facing Tiger. The Beings of three were still positioned just as they had been all along. The atom that was still in front of me instantaneously expanded to a size where we were all within the void of the atom, between the nucleus and the electrons.

For readers who aren't aware of how the particles in an atom are divided, here's a quick explanation: Protons are particles with a positive (+) electrical charge, while neutrons, aptly named, have no electrical charge. Those two types of particles are found in the nucleus, or core of the atom. Electrons are negatively (-) charged particles that orbit the nucleus of the atom at extremely high speed.

This + and − charge creates a fine balanced dance that allows for the existence of the atom. (The cloud formation of electrons encircling the atom currently being witnessed would be a dimensional wake, so to speak, that the electrons create in what would be once removed.)

Tiger's thoughts told me to take notice of the electrons zipping around above us, then instructed me to direct all my attention and awareness on an individual electron. Keep in mind that as soon as I thought or felt anything the Teachers and Tiger were aware of it instanteneously. This is the exact connection we each share here in the physical world, but have over the years switched it off completely.

Tiger instructed me to direct the selected electron down in front of myself. With the electron at what would be arms' length away, I was then asked to release it from thought. The electron began, slowly at first, to revolve around me at roughly chest height. It was here where I first fully became aware and experienced a 360 degree perception and consciousness. I could see the electron at all times, never losing awareness of it as it revolved around me.

The electron created an "e-motion" (electricity initiates motion) within me that, to this day, I have been unable to express coherently. Suffice it to say that I felt as though the electron was a significant part of what I truly am.

Tiger then instructed me to bring the electron to a stationary point once again in front of me. We were still positioned in the void of the atom, as Tiger went on to explain that it is this particle that is of greater importance than the central core of the atom. The electron itself is the stabilizing factor of the physical universe, and a larger part of what we as physical Beings do not yet understand. As his thoughts transferred to me, he went on to explain that without electrons the nucleus would destabilize. Then as his thoughts discontinued, the electrons of the large scale atom we were in suddenly disappeared and the nucleus flew apart at such a tremendous velocity, they merely vanished.

The negatively charged electrons stabilize atoms' cores by confining the positively charged nuclei to their central location, thus creating the over all structure of the atom. The oscillating, chaotic dance performed by the protons and neutrons at the nucleus of the atom truly is a factor of the magnetic force of electrons at work. As you can also see, without electrons there would be no atoms, and with no atoms there is no physical reality – period. *In that scenario though the Beings we truly are at our core would still exist.*

The central core or nucleus of an atom also has its own dimensional structure to bring it into being. Though not as important, quarks, gluons (dry cake ingredients) and other particles come together to form those protons and neutrons. The quarks and gluons etc. are what would be considered of a dimension one step removed from the physical atom.

The importance of electrons being the spark to all there is goes beyond the fact they are the stabilizers of the known physical universe as they are the basis of raw electricity. This is the very same electricity that runs nearly everything we use in our modern world. From the computer I am sitting at, to the light you are more than likely reading by, electrons provide the energy that makes them work. Taking that a step further, not only do the computer and light run on electricity, but the physical aspects and structure of both are also *made of* electricity, by way of their atom/atomic beginnings. Though your physical body may genetically have a lot in common with a chimpanzee, the essence of what you truly are within that body, has more in common with the electricity running through your power cords.

Once the fact is understood that all things physical start at a non-physical dimension of a sub-atomic, electrical point, you begin to see what we are. It is more fully realized that both aspects of our person, physical and non-physical are electrical in nature at their very foundations. The ramifications of that fact start to take shape once you come to understand the finer details. The oscillations of both our physical person and non-physical essence is the direct effect of that electricity, which creates magnetic fields as well as frequencies. Your thoughts, feelings, raw e-motions, as well as physical actions are directly linked back to that spark of electrons.

Upon birth, an innate knowing resides within each one of us, though it's the focus of orienting ourselves within this physical world that has distracted us so much that we've simply forgotten. Our original need to integrate the essence and foundation of what we are into this physical world reality forced us to forget and now has become that internal yearning to know. The lack of proper integration by way of truly understanding with clarity both aspects of what we are as well as who we are drives us to know and understand once again.

Since the beginning of human history, there has existed an internal knowledge that something seems to be missing. So many have searched for so long to know the truth about what we each are. The search is not necessarily for proof, though perhaps on the surface it has always seemed to be exactly that. Having had the NDE experience and marveled at all that was, all that is and all that will be, I now know it to have always been more of a search for understanding. A true, dot-connected-to-dot understanding, to create a new beginning from which each of us can step forward.

The statement *"Be the Light that you are and that you want to see in the world"* is oh so much more true than you may realize, as electrons create and emit the photons that are light. So Be the Light that you truly are.

CHAPTER 7

From Here To There Is....Oh So Close

"I can only become to mean as much as what I do for others"

—Alan R. Stevenson

Lesley wrote in to say:

Thank you for sharing your enlightening story. I helped my father transition on May 31st 2009 for 4 days and it was a very enlightening experience. I was also able to communicate and know that my beloved grandparents were there to greet him so he was not going to be alone.

Love, Light & Compassion Now & Always!

It was by the very simple act of slipping from my biological glove that I came to understand so much, as the supposed veil between the two dimensional worlds had been lifted. The lesson learned was that the tangible world is made and comprised from the essence of the intangible. The demarcation or transitional point we've come to believe in does not exist. The existence of such a belief is due largely to our inability to fathom the initial components of our physical world/reality. Much in the same way, during ancient times, the linear thinking principle created a drop off point at the edge of the world for seafarers. Our need to relate to things by way of our personal and/or common life experience becomes paramount in our ability to be okay with that which we accept. The need to do so coupled with our linear mode of thinking creates a Chinese paper finger trap that so many get stuck in.

Prior to my heart attack I, just as you more than likely do, perceived my physical self and surroundings as the hard, solid fact that they are. Even if you do believe in and know that we're a Soul based Being, you've probably had a hard time putting a finger on the finite actuality of that. Before my heart attack, I experienced a solid form of life. During my NDE, I experienced another form of existence, and post heart attack I saw and experienced the coalescence of the two.

I actually started putting several things together later on the day of my heart attack. The first thing I came to realize was that where our essence of Being comes from is only one step removed from this physical dimension. I briefly outlined this in the previous chapter as the last leg of atomic particles combining to begin the structural formation of physical matter. That would be "the other side", or the cake batter stage, if you will. At the beginning of chapter three I also mentioned an interaction of my hands and fingers with faint, yet continual, shadow-like objects while I was still in the hospital.

I want to come back to that point for a moment, as it was the first time I witnessed anything like it. The non-physical interacting with physical aspects of the world around me was a new and unique experience. While in hospital and prior to extending my arms out to the furthest point of my peripheral vision, I thought there might be something wrong with my eyesight as a result of the heart attack. As I mentally contemplated the possibility that this might be a permanent after-effect, I came to an emotional balance point. While still dancing in the magic of being alive, I decided that it was a better-than-okay trade off. It is such a shame, though, that we must lose or come close to losing something so treasured before we fully appreciate it as we should from the start. That life lesson was quickly learned that day.

With my arms nearly straight out from my shoulders, what I witnessed in the hospital bed that first evening was an interaction of the non-physical with my physical body. At first, the faint objects were merely darting from the edge of my vision, to about 45 degrees from the center of my eyesight, then vanishing. That occurred only until I reached out with my arms. Though many of the objects continued to pass by in a near blur-like fashion, several started to flow along my arms, hands and fingers. At one point while I was doing this, one of the ICU nurses came out from behind the nurse's station, heading straight for my room. I pulled my arms in trying to make it look as though I was just stretching. Upon entering she asked if I was alright or was I experiencing any pain. With amazement swirling within, a perplexed smile was all I could muster in reply to her simple question.

Shortly after she left the room, I reached out with only my left arm. The objects once again started to float and flow around my hand and fingers, creating a bit of a tingling sensation. The electrical energy that was being transferred flowed right straight through me to the central core of my Being. I was only able to see the objects as long as I kept the center of my vision angled away a bit, just as I had to with the Beings of 111 during my NDE. This interaction went on for at least a good hour, after which from nowhere I felt a strong urge to get out of bed and walk around for the first time since that morning.

Though I do not know what or who the objects were, to this day I believe that what I'd been witnessing was a unique and special healing taking place. I say this because several weeks later during testing they could not find any cellular damage to my heart of any kind, which should not have been possible, due to the severity of the heart attack.

Shortly after the interaction took place, a couple of the dots from the lessons I was taught started connecting and clicking into place. I saw in my mind a large, clear glass bowl being pushed down into some foamy, soap-suds-filled dish water. Through the glass bowl, I could see the contents at the bottom of the sink. The bowl sat far enough down into the water that the foam was up around its very edge. Our eyesight, when peering into physical reality, works a lot like this in regard to dimensional aspects. You only need to become a bit more aware of the outer area of your vision to start to take notice of things. For most, the electrical energy of our thoughts is so narrowly focused to the small, central point of our vision that we become oblivious to so much. Some of you, though, may have at one time or another seen something move out at the edge of your vision and turned to look, only to find nothing there. This very thing happened to me continually for several months after getting out of the hospital and has now resurfaced once again.

Let's go back to our cake batter stage of particles combining for a moment. This batter stage of the cake baking would be considered the other side in the overall scheme of things. As you well know and can see, it doesn't look a single bit like the finished cake, now does it? We also know, however, that once it goes through that final process of baking, it will transform. What we have a hard time with is the point at which the batter is the cake and the cake was the batter as a reference.

I don't want to over-complicate things here, but there is little else I can do to explain it. I've sat for long periods of time, trying to come up with a way to show, rather than simply tell it. The problem with our comprehension of atomic structure is the points at which we can and can't see it, just as in the cake and batter scenario. The components or ingredients have to come together enough to become physical in structure, BUT just prior to doing so, they are still considered to be "the other side".

Here is one more analogy to help those who may not have baked a cake from scratch. Have you ever gone about sweeping a floor that for all intents and purposes looked fairly clean? You go about dragging the broom over the kitchen floor and by the end of doing so have a nice little collection of stuff you couldn't initially see. You can see in this example that, once the tiny little stuff is brought together, something more substantial comes into being. As you go about bringing together all the other floor sweepings from room to room, you have something even more substantial.

As the soul slips from the biological glove of the body, it is already on the other side. This is where the essence of deceased loved ones resides. I believe you are coming to a point of realizing and understanding how oh-so-close your passed-on loved ones actually are. The electrical energy of what they are is just at the edge of the spectrum on a wavelength we can't quite perceive, at least almost all of us. People like Theresa Caputo, John Edwards and many others are very close to that edge themselves with what they are soulfully. The deceased Beings can affect the electrical aspects of electrons and other subatomic particles from their realm that traverse the supposed veil into physical reality as a current. Theresa and others pick this up as an image within their mind and essence of their own soulful Beings to relay the messages they do. The concept is somewhat like the electrical data that flows from a computer hard drive to become a printer hard copy.

The only real difference between a live human being and a deceased one is the energetic flow of electricity, or current, that animates biology. You may or may not have had the opportunity to view a deceased being or even wished to for that matter, but one truly important fact stands out. The person or personality and animated characteristics you've come to know as Dick, Jane, Bobby or Betty are no longer present.

Think of you and your car for a moment, as the two separate objects they are, in a scenario in which you are your soul and the car is your physical body. Think of how, as your physical, total self sitting down in your car, strapping in and shutting the door, you come to a different perception. The same is also true when stepping out of your car. Now, how we, as individuals, drive our cars / physical lives, is an altogether different thing.

You can, with a bit of awareness, learn to listen, understand, and receive those messages from deceased loved ones yourself. Most people who have "lost" a person from their immediate inner circle can periodically sense that person in different ways. We each have our very own soulful as well as biological radar systems built right in. If you've ever felt a warm hum or buzz on your arms, or the hair on the back of your head stood up, you'll understand what I'm saying. This typically is your essence and biology reacting to electrical stimulation only once removed dimensionally from your current physical reality. The "departed" loved one has merely returned to being that energetic current which is the exact same foundation of our physical biology at a sub-level. This is the point at which we, as the soulful Beings we actually are, click into, or out of our bodies, just as the ski boot clicks to the ski, becoming a part of the ski.

Typically we are unaware of the subliminal imagery that forms within us during a verbal conversation with another person. The imagery itself is so we may comprehend what is being said, and to reply if need be. However when a departed loved one tries to make contact, their first and only real line of communication is by way of imagery. Nearly all auditory sounds from the other side sit outside of our normally tuned frequency range. Our current, overactive "fight or flight" systems dump in so much raw fear that we disconnect the incoming call from the departed. By merely understanding that they intend and can do no harm, along with a bit of practice you will be afforded the opportunity to potentially learn so much.

All that I am extends out in sorrow to those mothers, fathers, brothers and sisters who have lost a loved one. My only wish for you is that you find enough peace to allow them to let you know they are okay and now understand the loving peacefulness of their true essence.

To you Theresa, John and so many others that unceasingly help so many Beings get unstuck from the quicksand of life, or paralysis of a lost loved one, I humbly take my humble hat off !

CHAPTER 8

E=M
Electricity is Magnetic

> "Every tree has its branches, twigs, leaves or needles. Without them there would be no tree."
>
> —*Alan R. Stevenson*

Raewyn wrote to say:

I too have experienced a connection with the other side and it was a very overwhelming experience which came with a message, which proved to be correct back in 1989. A day I will never forget which started out as a walk in the park.

Namaste

There are times when things seem to be so very obvious and then there are those times when our perspective and perception blur the actuality of that which only seems obvious.

During one of the intermissions of the Hayhouse authors' conference at Roy Thomson Hall in Toronto, I met and was speaking with a couple of individuals who had asked some serious questions. After the two moved on, my line of sight connected with the eyes of a late 20's or early 30-something woman who had been waiting patiently, just behind the other two. Even though that contact was met with a smile, I felt as though a metal door had been slammed shut. I literary felt it! I quickly understood this person to be of a strong "bowling ball" personality (one of the types I'll define later). Stepping towards me with arms defiantly folded, stating "That's nothing! I know all about Atoms and that I'm made of atoms. Everybody knows that, and you just don't realize that everybody else already knows it." I felt the full force of her internal blast, but only for about a nanosecond. I softened up my magnetic field to be similar to that of the earth's protective magnetic shield billowing in the solar winds.

From that point on, none of her directed, electrically-based magnetic energy was able to affect me in any way shape or form. My electrical stream and peaceful frequency wasn't the slightest bit disrupted. Undaunted, I asked if she understood what her statement actually meant in the overall grand scheme of things. Though beginning to soften a bit, she quickly tossed back a few more firm, flippant remarks that had nothing to do with the question that was put forth. While she danced around all the direct questions, I realized she knew of the atom, understood we are made of atoms, but that's where it ended. I expressed, as soulfully as I could, that she was just as so many others are, to no fault of her own, yet still nothing more or less than another soul. As I maintained my soft field, it didn't take long for her tone - and head - to drop a bit. I asked the question once again, to help her realize the level of her misunderstanding, so that we could move forward.

During the more passive conversation that followed, the young woman commented how at different times during her life she'd done one thing or another and the specific outcome had been the opposite of what she had intended. She told me it left her perplexed and often very frustrated. We began to discuss the ramifications of the atom being what it is. By the time our interaction ended, her smile radiated. Thanking me, though still somewhat closed up, she walked away. Turning to walk away myself, a familiar sensation grew within. I stopped for a moment to look back in her direction, knowing she'd made a soft turn along the path on her own etch-a-sketch board of life.

Most of us are like this to a fair degree, perhaps not so much in regard to attitude, but more in terms of our knowledge and understanding of things. Let me try to illustrate the point. There are currently in the neighborhood of a billion computer users worldwide. Nearly all of those users clearly understand where the button to turn them on is, what the mouse, keyboard and monitor are for and how to use them. As with all things, there is a broad spectrum of knowledge and understanding from individual to individual when it comes to the overall group. Over 90% of all computer users only use a very small fraction of the potential capability of their computers. They stick to using them for a few very basic tasks, never understanding how much more they could be doing with them. The fundamental premise of that statement is also true about people's lives.

Today, the majority of members of our global society are getting a mere fraction of the true potential from their physical lives. This due totally to their beliefs, perception, and current understanding. Those beliefs, perceptions and understandings are fundamental to the construction of the life path each of us walks. During the course of a life, as an individual's understanding of things changes, so does the path that person walks. That deconstruction and re-structuring creates such an erratic path it is of little wonder why so many feel lost today.

Unfortunately, we receive our initial introduction to the atom at an age when our attention and focus is flowing in many other directions. With the exception of a few, we learn to dismiss what we learn, never realizing its significance. There are, however, some who, at various stages of life, come back to scratch their heads and wonder about the potential significance of the atom. These individuals try, desperately at times, to put a finger on the cause or reason for the often-frustrating meandering through life. They find themselves searching for the meaning of life rather than looking at what has been done and the results of those specific actions on all levels.

The term *"cause and effect"* may quickly come to mind, but in this case the elemental factors of the cause are misunderstood. This stems from our having been taught at a young age only the physical aspects of *"cause and effect,"* which we naturally implement a short while later into our lives. The physical points of view: "Touch a burner, you get burned." or "Miss the nail head with the hammer you hit your finger." are but surface factors. These situations, when witnessed by someone else create a sense and state of obviousness. This brings me back to the opening phrase of the chapter: "There are times when things seem to be so very obvious and then there are those times when our perspective and perception blur the actuality of that which only seems obvious."

There should be a clear understanding that at the elemental level there is nothing on this planet or in our lives that doesn't begin without the atom. The atom is the initial piece of the puzzle, however that piece itself also has pieces or components. We talked briefly earlier about those components, where the electron was the one which is of the most significant importance. It should also be understood that the electron is, for the most part, what could be referred to as raw electricity. It might also be noteworthy that, just as it takes a lot, and I mean a whole lot of water molecules to have running water, it also takes an incredible number of electrons to have flowing electricity as we understand it. For example, though roughly speaking I might add, a single ampere or more commonly known as an amp, consists of one million billion electrons, give or take a few, passing over a single point in one second. That makes it abundantly clear that they, the electrons, move along at a good clip. That said, I don't feel that it is of any real importance to go into depth about the other terms associated with gauging electrons and or electricity. I'll only mention them for possible reference. Those commonly known terms are as follows; volts, watts, ohms, coulombs and, of course, the ampere/amp.

There is an even more important aspect of electrons and electricity that, for most of my life, I didn't understand. This was due to a belief system I had, that electricity and magnetism were two separate entities. It was only later that I found out that you can't have one without the other, in a roundabout-way. On one hand they are separate, on another they are not. Confused? Don't worry, you will be, just as I was! I assure you, my intent is not to scare but to make you aware. The magnetic aspect of electricity is by far the single most important fundamental factor you must come to understand. We will walk slowly, but as briefly as possible through this information.

Since what I was shown during my NDE would make little sense to most people, I figured I'd look for a different way to explain that magnetics and electricity, as well as photons/light are actually only a part of the physics category. To avoid this piece becoming a dry portion of a physics text book, I will only touch on a few significant factors to give the gist of things. Should you wish to continue on with your own search into this, I commend you wholeheartedly. You shall more than likely, by the end, arrive back at the same point from which you began, just as I did. Let me explain. Maxwell's Laws/equations were created by one James Clerk Maxwell (1831-1879). JC was the first to bring together electricity, magnetism and light as a manifestation of the very same phenomenon. These Laws describe aspects of electricity, electrical fields, magnets and magnetic fields to which photons/light were added, to some degree, and for good reason. Then, at some later point in time, in steps the theory of Quantum Electrodynamics, which states electric & magnetic fields don't actually exist at all! This theory further states that all visible force is the result of charged particles exchanging photons/light with each other. That, I am sorry to say, I can not simplify. I did, however, mention at the end of chapter 5 that the light we visibly see is actually created by a process of the atom's electron, then emitted. I only reiterate it here as Dr. Wayne Dyer and so many others shine their light by discussing the light that you truly are. I am here to show and say that they are so very right. We all have seen someone glow radiantly at one time or another and you now understand how and why they do.

While diving into the scientific material, one of the first things I saw that was synonymous with events shown during my NDE, is that a single charged particle creates an electric field everywhere throughout the entire universe. Now, if you take that charged particle and enclose it in an object there are electric field lines that extend out from the particle. Think of it as a small Styrofoam ball for a moment. By filling the surface of the ball with kabob skewers, the electric field lines become a little more visually clear. The number of those skewers or electric field lines is determined only by the amount of the original charge of the particle. That was Maxwell's first Law of the four he wrote around 1861-62. By the way, those twelve-inch skewers we've been using to illustrate the field lines of flow actually extend out to infinity in all directions. I just thought you should know that as well as keep it in mind.

After reading and re-reading Maxwell's second Law several times, it got me wondering. First, though, I should state that electric fields are very different from magnetic fields. Primarily, the difference is in the process of how they operate or function. Maxwell's second Law states that the number of magnetic lines leaving a charged particle is ALWAYS ZERO. "Hmmm," so I scratched my head once again. A North pole particle and a South pole particle (a + and a -) will always attract one another. In essence, the positive particle's lines flow away while the negative particle's lines flow in. Taking into account that the two always attract, once joined together the lines flow out of one particle and directly into the other particle. Net zero, set and match, I think?

Maxwell's 3rd and 4th laws have little to do with this discussion but I should at least mention them. The third law states that the strength of a magnetic field around a loop depends strictly on the number of charged particles passing through the loop each second. The 4th law has to do with Ampere's Law and is an equation that relates to the static electric field around said closed loop. Those last two laws are, to the best of my understanding, more useful in understanding the principles of electric motors in use today.

Here are a few scientific statements for you to ponder. These are but some of the oddities you will find should you choose to look into them further for yourself.

1. Changing magnetic fields create electric fields and electric fields create magnetic fields which is a chain reaction known as a electromagnetic wave.

2. According to quantum mechanics, everything in the universe can behave as both a wave and/or a particle. At this point and perspective an electromagnetic wave is composed of particles of photons of light.

3. Nothing can travel faster through space than an electromagnetic wave. (The speed of light??? Just over 6,000,000,000,000 mpy = 1 light year) *Remember that the one Being said to me that the atom before you is as all others are!!!*

4. Bohr Model: When an electron drops in energy it emits a photon. – A photon is a bundle of energy / is a particle, though it isn't, nor is it a wave, but it might be a wave of particles. ????

5. Light is one of the least understood entities in physics. Hmmm?

6. Light is part of the Electromagnetic spectrum at or of a higher frequency than that of electric and magnetic fields/wave.

<u>The important things to keep in mind:</u>

Only spinning or moving particles create a magnetic field.

Every rotating charged particle is a miniature magnet!

In physical reality everything begins with the atom.

Atoms are balanced and made stable by electrons.

Electrons are electricity and have soft magnetic properties.

You are made of atoms as are all things physical.

Light comes from the electrons of atoms.

Magnetically, two Norths, Souths, positives or negatives will always repel or push away from each other.

A north and a south, or a negative and a positive will always attract one another. The same, or like, charge pushes, while opposite charges pull. Those last two are significantly involved with how we create our life and what we end up with.

Tiger's initial lesson, "It does not matter." helped me to learn the next lesson. Implementing that first lesson as a deflecting filter I was able to understand we are at a point where we can no longer step over a few simple facts and principles and need to become aware of them. Those facts and principles are the truth about the electric foundation of everything and how that works.

In the mere darkness, out in space or even in the depths of the ocean there's a point where direction becomes hard to comprehend, and so, too, does it in Life. So many people today are close to the surface waterline of all that they are and could be, yet are unaware of their actual positioning as they stare down into the depths of the water below. The disorienting contradictions we see, feel and experience in our lives are, as you can see, also expressed in terms of what science wrestles with continually.

CHAPTER 9

The Art of Being
What I've learned

*"Toss fear aside and be genuine in all that you do
and those you meet will know
the Soul you truly are."*

—Alan R. Stevenson

Patti wrote in to say:

Thank you so much for writing this Alan. What an amazing experience, and what a gift it is to others! One of my former bosses passed on at the age of 37 from breast cancer. In the moment before she transitioned, she said to her mom and husband, "Oh my God—they're here!" It was as if she had seen angels or people she knew.

The mother of my next boss also had a wonderful experience before she moved on. With the family around her hospital bed, she said, "There's a line—they're telling me to cross the line." The family encouraged her to cross the line, and she transitioned.

Your experience must have been incredible. Your work here was not done. You will help many people—giving hope and peace around living and dying—before you have the opportunity to move on again.

Thank you so very much for all you are doing.

Namaste.

By dictionary definition, the word "Being" takes on a life of its own, yet creates a reasonably clear path to understand its foundational basis: Existing; existence (as opposed to nonexistence), conscious, mortal existence; life: "Our being is as an instantaneous flash of light in the midst of eternal darkness." Substance or nature, something that exists: *inanimate beings.* A living thing, and last but not least, a human being; person. Then, on the philosophical side there is, a./ that which has actuality either materially or in idea, and b./ absolute existence in a complete or perfect state lacking no essential characteristic; that being the *essence* of. (dictionary.com)

An initial contradiction of our existence, is that for most people, it isn't until after departing this physical realm that they truly come to know or get the chance to fully comprehend the Art of Being. It is, however the lesson of "Being" in a physical world that we have yet to learn. Our blind spots are many and knowledge of what is truly important remains so very rare. Much in the same way that we know little about and do not understand death, the same is also true as to what we honestly understand about Life. We continue trying desperately to get to that point of simple understanding. We constantly struggle to know what we are, to understand who we are, and why we are here in the first place. Along with that, we want to know what we are to do with this amazing thing called Life and how we are to be while we're here.

So many people today feel the internal, core feeling that life is not as it was supposed to be, inherently knowing there is something far grander than us all at work. However, there are individuals who believe that we're doing fine as a race of Beings, saying, "We've managed to survive so far." Furthermore, with simple observation, the obvious reply is, "Have we not?!" We hold a belief based on our advancements in technology and science, etc. These still are, however only aspects of the physical world, having little to do with the importance of what you are within. Then, at the end of a life, in those last hours and moments we finally come to learn those things have little to do with what is actually important. The reality in which we exist, due to its seemingly solid nature, literally forces us to bypass our innate sense of knowing and Being during our lives.

It is apparent that I'm no longer who I originally thought myself to be prior to being shown what I am. To suddenly realize that I was not what I believed myself to have always been created a greater realization, that our current perception of life is very limited and backwards to its actuality. The limitations are similar to looking at some beautiful scenery through a pinhole in a large wall. Unfortunately, we never become aware the wall exists, or at least not in its truest sense. We think and have come to believe that what we see through that infinitesimal hole is all there is. Just as so many others, I had to literally arrive at that extreme point and those last few moments of life to desperately reach for what is important. In those last moments, I finally learned that the only things of any true value are intangible.

However, the backward point of view that physical life is our primary existence, to which there is a soul attached in some form must be reversed. The sub-level ethereal Being you *"are"* must come first, then the physical Being of *"who"* you have become is finally clear and appreciated for what it is. Knowing first that there is a difference, then truly understanding what the difference between the two is, your path shall unfold. With proper understanding your innate knowledge will present itself and you'll no longer be separate and estranged from everything there is. A time is upon us to understand what it means to be the Being, and all that you truly are. Life, death, living & dying, however are all different components of Being.

There is something so truly wondrous about who each individual human being has become during their life. I have seen much and experienced even more, enough to know we are all miracles. The mere fact of your physical presence and absolute Being is genuinely miraculous to begin with. Perhaps there is a way I can show you this, and not just the reflection you believe you're aware of.

Since your Soul's consciousness existed long before your physical self, I'd like you to relax for a moment and in that state of consciousness step back just previous to your physical self.

Now allow your physical existence to flow forward as though a bud on the stem of a flower, unfolding to full bloom. For the next moment, if you consider all that needed to take place for you to have arrived at this point, here and now, there should ensue an e-motionalized sense and physical feeling of that miraculous nature. Physical Life, however deals its cards in odd ways to each one of us, as we experience the profound contradiction of existence. In this state, Life is so unimaginably resilient in regard to so many different aspects of physically being, yet we see, e-motionalize, feel, and experience just how fragile it can be in the same breath.

Our sense and understanding of the physical world brings us to separate ourselves from it. At times, we look with total awe and amazement at what nature has given us, as well as what humankind has created. Be it a statue freed a thousand years ago from it's encapsulated state of a million years, or perhaps a sunset while listening to the soft rush of waves we marvel at it. For others, however, it could be the roaring of a mud buggy through a bog. Regardless of what it is, while we look and feel it, we forget we're made of the exact same awe-inspiring stuff and every bit as amazing. Just as you've been awe-inspired by nature and the things you've witnessed, you have that same ability and essence within yourself, to stir that particular sensation of awe in all those you come to meet. You, - all that you are, is made of the same material as everything there is.

E+E = ME The Animator

More than anything else, I want to show you the awe-inspiring potential of the ability you possess. This state of Being has two elemental components, with the obvious being your physical body you've come to believe yourself to be. As you more than likely already know, your physical body's make-up begins with atoms. Then, there's the non-physical energy of what you are that animates that physical biology. Once that energy is withdrawn, however and completely detached from biology, biology is no longer animated, becoming the definitive point between being alive and not.

The only difference between a "Being"/person who is alive and one that is not, is the flow of electrical current throughout that physical biology. The truth is that you are a subatomic-level, conscious Being positioned within a molecular-level, atomic-based structure, where both are balanced, as well as governed by, electrons or electricity. Soul pushes buttons, flicks switches, pulling and pushing levers via the brain, as it's the console or interface through which Soul navigates and participates in this purposeful physical life experience.

Just as you mesh the fingers of one hand with the fingers of your other hand, Soul integrates with your physical biology at a foundational sub-level, equally shared by both Soul and biology. Soul climbs into the driver's seat, so to speak, so you can experience, learn, grow, and evolve.

Prior to stepping back from the other side, I was taught, and after my NDE learned, that the internal unrest we feel stems simply from our believing we do not know. Just as the colorblind person cannot see a pattern of specifically-colored dots among other dots, we seemingly cannot see the answers that lie within us all. Here, in our physical reality, multiple e-motional states create a roller coaster ride that none of us were meant to be on.

My NDE allowed me to bask in the environment that our essence of Being originates in, of only one e-motion - a verbally indescribable Love . You have all the Love you will ever need within you, in all that you are and the fact you are connected always, in all ways to the heavenly dimensional realm. You need only realize this simplest of truths first.

So, search not externally, outward from yourself. Find the Love within what you are, to allow it to blossom within, and then unfold as the flower does, spreading its seeds. This Love becomes apparent in each of the individuals we meet and come to know, as well as those close to us.

> "Fall in Love with Life...
> and you shall be in Love for your entire Life."
>
> —*Alan R. Stevenson*

If you can start to realize that all there is, is the electricity of electrons, you begin to understand that the little things such as your thoughts (electrical), voice (frequency), E-motions (electrical current flowing over atomic biological matter), physical actions (electrical current producing frequency), affects all that is around you and all who you know. If there is electricity, there must be a magnetic field present. We constantly are pushing and pulling each other around, unknowingly affecting one another's lives.

When you worry fearfully about a loved one in regard to situations that probability has already pushed to the outer framework of being a remote chance, you bring it back into the realm of having a high potential of happening. Once you learn how we create and affect the unfolding of our moments to come, that last statement shall be better understood. Our very own, self-defeating e-motional states pour out at the most inopportune times in such a rush and flow that our true abilities to simply do as we know we can never gets the chance to merge with that high-speed traffic. On the other hand, it never ceases to amaze me what we can actually accomplish when we remain balanced, clear and focused on what we are doing.

Why are we afraid of change? We fear that what we physically are and the life we've become okay with will change, yet what we truly are cannot. However, who we have become will change, just as it always has and will continue to do throughout our lives, though gradual and unnoticed in the short term. Throughout life, the things we think and e-motionalize end up sticking to us like glue (magnetically), which creates the life problems we all encounter. At times, we become frustrated and angry, taking things out on those around us in an unconscious, manipulative manner. This, in turn, creates more core-based frustrations in others, usually those closest to us and often the ones we love. A mere thought is more damning than a physical action can be in most situations, for it is the beginning point which brings to bear all the energy & forces we are. We do it, however with little understanding. What is right or wrong in one culture in some part of the world is not in another part of the world. The only common way for us all to Be is that of the Loving origin we come from.

> *" It is the Being within the person
> that accounts for all things along the path."*
>
> —Alan R. Stevenson

At one time or another, we have all come to a point of having spoken from a core e-motion, speaking passionately, lovingly, from a sense of joyfulness, through what we are. Predominately, though, we turn off our awareness and speak or act with little thought, and just as the fire devastatingly roaring through the forest, it all started with a mere ember of e-motionally-triggered thought to ignite so much destruction. The process is similar to the GUN, TRIGGER, BULLET effect. We act first, with the justification of Being able to say we're sorry after the fact. That is not unlike pulling the trigger of a gun, then trying to stop the bullet once it has left the barrel, or believe that saying sorry will repair the ripping damage of the bullet. We must learn to Soulfully e-motionalize, think, physically feel, then do, arriving at a correct response to a situation.

Time and time again throughout our lives, we experience the hesitant fear of doing something new. After going through a new situation or experience, however the first thing that usually comes to mind is, " Now, that wasn't so bad." You can learn to express varying e-motional aspects in a physical manner, without the internal roller coaster ride, once you differentiate the two. E-motional flow and waves dictate physical animated response, yet do not need to. Once you learn to stand still and remain peaceful while a freight train goes by, nearly brushing your left shoulder and a bomb goes off just to your right at the same time, you will be where you should be. I understand that from your perspective, it is easier said than done, yet if you carry Tiger's first lesson of " It does not matter" with you, situations shall dissolve long before a fire starts to roar.

> "The peace you seek is within...
> So you are never truly without"

Every master of a given skill, such as a surgeon, computer tech, race car driver, painter, sculptor, writer or singer, worked at what they do to be the absolute best they can be. We all have the same foundation of Being and it is up to us to work at and on it. We must learn to be that much better - not than another being, but from our own current level of understanding. It is through awareness and then work that this is achieved.

> "MONEY can't fix a busted Soul"
>
> —*Alan R. Stevenson*

Holding on & Letting go. "I went from what I was to what I am with little left of who I was." As a child, when a toy is lost or broken and then replaced, it never seems to have the same feel as the original, due to our underlying attachment. As adults, we experience the same effect in many different ways. This stems from our attachment to things of physical reality. Seeing them for what they are makes the lesson of letting go, which is an aspect that must be learned, easier to do because we remember what is of true value and importance.

> "A factor of your path...
> Give always, ask for nothing &
> then watch the magic of a day unfold."

Physical life truly is like that Etch-a-Sketch board... You choose to turn, or you choose to go straight, being all that which you have become, due to your original choice to "Be". So, rejoice in your choice. Neal Donald Walsh, author of *Conversations with God*, spoke of and alluded to the fallible nature of being human, which I would like to reiterate. There truly are NO MISTAKES when choosing which way to turn at any given moment or situation, only a path from which to learn. To learn is to ask the what & why of yourself, just as you did of your parents, when once a child.

Sharon wrote in to say;

I was intrigued because I had a personal experience with a being of light, and she (I call it a she but really, there was no sex) had a companion. The being was of pure light energy and total love and acceptance and approval. I wanted to sit in her presence forever. The companion did not have that intensity of pure love, and the closest I can describe the companion was like a personal assistant standing next to the main body of Pure Light of Love... but... neither had form, just energy. You are the first account that describes a dominant or central being, with "companions". If not for my "proof", I would have concluded after all these years that it was just a dream. I was not given messages but I was left with a feeling of knowledge for me. So nope, no message that mankind was on a precipice and or a mission to keep mankind from ruining themselves. BUT, I was left with an overwhelming awareness that LOVE was the ONLY thing that mattered. And my life has had that theme ever since. I share that message of LOVE, even though I rarely discuss my woowoo experience. I was not a bad person on a bad path. But I was living shallow, doing good work (interventional cardiology which you know about!), but not really thinking of life or humanity or anything. Just working/eating/sleeping, repeat repeat.

I am interested in the messages you came back with. I have wondered if there was something wrong with me that I wasn't given messages. I was just left feeling a sense of purpose, to live life with LOVE as my core value.

Thank you for responding. I look forward to your book publishing.

Kind regards,

Dear Sharon; You did receive your most important and valuable message - having been given the understanding of your purpose and to live Life through the essence of your origin.

With the recent passing of Dr. Wayne Dyer, I wish to impress the importance of the statement I've made several times and only recently discovered that Wayne Dyer did as well. This statement is a fact of Being as well as the foundation of Being.

It is not for us or anyone to judge another soul in any way shape or form. If you think or feel you are more or less than another Being, you need to properly e-motionalize that within yourself, for it is merely an aspect of a way you have learned to Be - a way that society has taught. There exists no difference from one Soul Being to another, as the differences we perceive are just another one of the many illusions conceived by the parameters of our physical reality. Not even minutely does the strength from Being to Being differ within each of us, yet it is the perception of and expression of that essence that does. Where you place yourself in thought and e-motion, you are placed within the physical world society. That society should be of a neutral, harmonious nature, but is severally imbalanced, due to our disbelief in ourselves.

> "When you judge another
> You do not define them
> you define yourself."
>
> —Dr. Wayne Dyer

This unsettling imbalance has sent so many off on a spiritual quest to try and piece together enough truths to carry on. One must watch and be careful, as so many of what are believed to be spiritual concepts, are but mere parallel, mirror images. To illustrate this, consider yourself as a white cue ball at one end of a pool table representing your life. The target ball, your objective, sits just outside of a pocket on the opposite end. Your goal is to tap the ball precisely enough to knock it into the pocket, completing your spiritual quest. On that pool table, if you're out so much as a millimeter at the start of your quest or objective, you end up being two inches out once your ball/you have travel the length of the table/duration of your life, only to end up missing the target. While traveling one of those near-parallel lines, however, you believe your ball or yourself to be on the correct course. The difference between the proper spiritual path and one of the many others, is but an illusionary, mirror image, because they are so close together. The meaning of spirituality is an initial awareness that you are so much more than what you have become and believe yourself to be. It is to live in no judgement by no judgement, as it is about forgiving, and not forsaking. Though it is so much more than being that simple, it is the starting point upon your pool table.

We are born into a set frequency at which we operate. I know that when I came back, they reset mine to a different, higher one. Our essence, our Soul or that which we are slips into an atomic structure, so as to exist, experience and endure the physical construct. This is similar to the way a hand in a furnace has no chance, yet can endure for a time if in a fireproof glove. All there is, including you and I, is made of the exact same stuff, and that stuff resides also between us. Though I have not touched you, I can sense you, as all that there is, is electricity that becomes like phone lines through which thoughts traverse.

Your tomorrow is unpredictable only if you allow it to be, by way of simply not doing. When we are doing as we should, a peacefulness is granted. May you strive to be the true artisan of the Being you already are.

"When you become amazed with Life...
Amazing things begin to Happen."

—Alan R. Stevenson

CHAPTER 10

The Frankenstein Syndrome

*"We create our moments and time to come,
either by knowing and purposefully
or by default mode."*

—Alan R. Stevenson

Cheryl wrote in to say;

"Hi Alan! I do not know you. I became intrigued by your statement and read about the transforming chapter of your life event. Thank you for sharing your experience. My life has been visited by death of loved ones in the past several years. Most recent, Feb. 2008 my Mother. Mar. 2009, my Sister. As strange as this may sound Alan, I have been somewhat preoccupied...with death. I thought death was suppose to be so...final. Your story depicted just the opposite. I have heard of people dying and then, given another chance at life. It seems individuals each have their own experience. I do believe events take place that surpass all human understanding. I think I get what you mean by us having a choice... being empowered if we CHOOSE to B. I like that Alan! May I say, I am glad you decided to stay."

There are not too many people who haven't at least heard of Mary Shelley's epic novel *"Frankenstein"*, which she penned in 1818 at the tender age of only 20. The thing I find very interesting is that if you ask five different people what the baseline of the story is, there will typically be five different responses. Though there may be some similarities, in the end they're so different and just as varied as the individuals. As for myself, I figured the story was of a doctor with some good intentions, but a few bad - very bad - ideas. His worst idea was to piece many different parts together, and then re-animate that which was no longer alive. The doctor's focused objective, however, was a failure as he created a monster rather than what he'd originally envisioned.

I fully realize it may seem a bit odd or perhaps even bizarre that I'd use such a tale to make a point in a spiritual-type book. If you bear with me for a moment, though, I'm sure you'll come to fully understand why. There's nothing sinister intended here, as we ourselves are no different than the good doctor himself. Dr. Frankenstein wished to create life and make it better. How could that desire have anything to do with yourself? Well, although the doctor wanted to create an individual life form... oh, but wait a minute! Is it not the life of an individual we're creating? Are we not doing the exact same thing, moment by moment, day in and day out, with our very own lives and the path we walk?

Another element we share with the doctor are the monsters/situations we inadvertently create on a daily basis, though never understanding why. I'm not suggesting we actually turn something into a living, breathing, physical being that is a monster; that's not it at all. Yet, just like the doctor, we start with good intentions in attempting to create our lives, but more times than not, end up with the opposite of our initial desires. Dr. Frankenstein had a concept, a fair amount of knowledge, stacks of books, lots of experience with life, and a strong desire to do good. What he lacked, though, was the proper way in which to bring his concepts to life in the way he intended them. We, ourselves are so very much like this, in that we sense we're capable and have within us the know-how to create our lives. Just like the word that eludes us at an inopportune time, only to hang at the tip of our tongues, so too does our vague understanding of how to create the life we want. Then, only at a later point in time does the answer come to us, just like the word that finally pops into our minds, minutes or hours later.

Something deep within drives us onward to succeed at having the life we desire, yet we continue to stumble. The cycle persists time and time again, because of the separation of the proper knowing how to do and the doing. With the passage of time, we invariably become frustrated with the concept of taking hold of the controls to steer our lives in the direction we want. Once the multitude of attempts at different concepts fail, we unconsciously switch back to our internal auto-default mechanism for creating our lives. For the vast majority of individuals, this is true. If you look around a bit, even within your own circle of people, you'll see many with their auto-pilot turned on.

There are, however, those Beings out there who've proven that with a big enough hammer they can make a square peg fit through a round hole. Over the past twenty-five plus years there have been so many well-intentioned concepts and ideas meant to help us create and then construct the lives we all internally wish for. Having a crude sense of the Soulful Being that lurks within, we read a mountain of books in search of a clearer understanding. Those books, however, have been written by others who've read an even larger mountain of books and studied more programs than you can count. A large portion of the books you've read may have ignited a soul-warming experience, which is good, as it is a start.

Perhaps in the past you've tried to implement some of what you've read, or something from a course you completed. It is here that you switched up to a bigger hammer or perhaps found what you had created was more of a monster than what you had intended. Though we do *attract* the components or pieces of the puzzle to our moments to come, we do not *attract* overall situations. From out of the mist of time, just moments ahead of us, our life unfolds. It unfolds in a manner where we create our situations by the way in which we perceive those components as well as the way we piece the puzzle together. Every minute element of what we desire is available to each and every one of us. The picture upon our finished puzzle created by us differs, however, from Being to Being. What is done with those pieces is due to the result of perception, from individual to individual, and that makes all the difference!

By becoming more consciously aware of the individual pieces, you won't continually need an increasingly bigger hammer to make the pieces of the puzzle fit. We've all seen that person sitting at a table, building a puzzle, then banging down with a fist because a piece really looks as though it should fit. Life situations are also like this, where so many force fit the pieces of life because they look as though they should fit.

It is here that most people get in their own way of allowing things to transpire. Being forceful in a physical manner to achieve a desired life goal runs totally against the intended gracefulness of life. All things that are, such as your life, and you, yourself have a natural, free-flowing, almost magical essence to them. Though perhaps seldom, we each have experienced miraculous moments during our lives - moments where the heavens and harmonious cosmos aligned and the tumblers seemed to click into place. However, once the auto-pilot of living life has been turned on, all the magic, beauty, love and grace of your true ability can not be experienced. At least not until you switch it off.

Searching for the answers you seek is just like trying to start a fire. The search itself to learn and the objects used, by way of the books read or courses taken, have become your igniters. Rubbing a couple of these concepts together, you see some sparks happening and immediately think and feel that you're on the right track. Inevitably, though, at some point down the road you're not willing to give up the hope you cling to of fulfilling your objective of starting that fire. I mean it makes perfect sense; you've got sparks flying and believe that at some point your fire, or should I say that for which you search, is going to catch and ignite the blaze.

Unfortunately, so many people today search outside themselves for the answers to life's mysteries when the answers lay within each one of us. Even after much reading and learning, the majority of those searching for a clearer understanding continue to feel their way around as though in darkness, and are still left wanting. They continue searching out in the physical because we are a physical Being and this life we live is a physical life. That mindset is physical reality's common sense beckoning you, while having little to do with the Being you are. Our physical selves are similar to the sealed glass bottle of air, but we see and focus only on the container, neglecting the unseen, true life force within.

Throughout life in this physical reality we constantly sidestep what is natural to us. This is done because we continue to think from within our lifelong conditioning that things must be much harder than they truly are. While I was back at home on the *other side*, I learned and truly realized at the core of all that I am, that life is much simpler. The truth is that we create effortlessly, at will, through our natural state of Being, while in the non-physical dimension of the *other side*. If you think of a place, you immediately go to that place, no matter where it might be. If you think of and truly feel something within yourself, it is there before you. This is creation, as it were, in the purest sense. Understand that the *other side* is just as it is here in this physical reality, yet without substance. Another truth is that our physical reality also has very little substance.

Even though the actual difference between the two dimensions is minute, a conscious barrier has still been set in place. The illusion of our realm's physicality creates that difference between the other side and here. That slight difference, however, makes for a time lag we forget to accept. Let me illustrate this in a different manner for you. Think of a large in-ground swimming pool. On land, along side the pool, you can walk or run with little resistance. But when you're chest deep in the water of the pool, it isn't so easy. The land represents the non-physical dimension, while in the water represents our physical realm.

Although the base foundation of the here and now is made of the same stuff as the other side, the physicality of this structural reality naturally inhibits the speed at which things occur. Hence, we easily become disillusioned with the progress of our efforts and methods to create. We then have a tendency to jump from method to method on a quest that never brings you back to the original, instinctual knowing within, of how we create.

We shall momentarily get into the missing keys to the vehicle of how we create, but to begin, one must first learn to drop the linear perspective. To visualize and understand that statement, as I said earlier, "Our physical reality is so much more from the inside out." I also mentioned the way in which to perceive this fact, and that is to see within your mind the concept of transforming from bud to blooming flower – which perfectly demonstrates how our future moments unfold before us.

Dr. Frankenstein achieved a portion of his desired goal, yet never stopped to consider the fundamental factor of whether it would end well or as badly as it did. The same is true when it comes to giving life to our own desired moments to come. It's just that the Key element of Life is misunderstood!

I Had to Die to Learn How to Live

CHAPTER 11

Architects We Are

"Remember; when you think of something good or bad, the non-physical universe begins to put it together for you. So always be mindful of your thoughts and more importantly your e-motions as they provide an energy to bring to life what you have architecturally drafted in thought form."

—*Alan R. Stevenson*

Steph Van De Ven Author of the Birdy Book wrote;

"You're amazing Alan! Your story will change hearts and souls all over the country. Thank you for being such a strong light in much darkness. Lots of love."

When most people think of an architect, they get the image of a person pushing and moving rulers around on their tilted tables and dragging a pencil along the ruler's edge. In reality, an architect truly is much more than just a pencil pusher. Well, at least in the old days, pre-computer age. Architects are a creative catalyst where desired concepts, ideas and e-motional content are fused together as a rendered, finished object. They take all the elements from an individual to create something that equals or exceeds that person's expectations. The architect's job is but half finished once he or she has laid down the pencil, having completed the drawings and blueprints. The architect then must form an alliance with the builder to ensure their ornately crafted drawings are followed with precision and precisely as intended. In the overall process of building, the architect is the bridge between mere ideas and those ideas becoming a reality.

Each day of your life, you architecturally design, draft and help build the life that is ever unfolding before you, either knowingly or unconsciously in an auto-default mode.

I was doing my best prior to the NDE to be optimistic and believe that life and my times to come were more than random occurrences, wherein the limits of my control over my own life were not confined to merely doing mundane, routine tasks - tasks that I performed only because they fell within the parameters of what I could do. My pre-NDE life was bound, just as many others are, to the cultivated guidelines of the small box of beliefs and existence. My box was designed with constraints that determined getting older and wiser only meant that I was adhering to the characteristics of the routine and adaptive animal we are.

> "It is from within ourselves that we ignite
> the magic each day holds, though the
> how and why is seldom understood."

Discovering the process in which we participate in creating the circumstances and structure of Life, dissolved the walls of that small box. This further altered every aspect of my understanding of Being, and my being within physical reality itself. The discovery and enlightenment of what I truly am and my potential to create and do as I wish, was by way of the Loving care of Tiger and the Beings of 111.

Now, to execute the creativity of the architect you are, in a skillful manner is going to take a fair bit of understanding. I assure you, though, you are more than capable of understanding. If a grade-ten high school dropout such as myself can understand and get it, I know you can as well. Before we go any further though, I need to take a moment to clarify that whenever I use the word "mind" in any form, I'm strictly referring to the consciousness of the Soul Being you are, within. First things first though, a few serious questions need asking, such as: "What is consciousness?" and "Where does consciousness reside?"

Many people have argued that thoughts originate in the brain. This unfortunate concept also furthers the notion of the finality of death, but I wish to illustrate some truth. Those that argue this line of reasoning are, however, on the same side of understanding that reasons that thoughts are consciousness itself. The understanding is that thoughts equate to being conscious, and with that I'm going to agree. However, the "From where does consciousness come?" as well as "Where does consciousness reside?" are questions that need to be answered.

Currently, there's an ever-growing number of reported cases and increasing evidence that consciousness survives the body and is not dependent upon the brain for its existence. That's been the divisional point: whether consciousness is of and stays with the body, or is in effect external to the body, leaving it at will. Many years ago, when there were only a few reported cases of NDEs, members of the science establishment were able to address those few and dismiss them abruptly. This created a cloud around any and all things that landed outside the framework of that small box that science said was the only definitive landing zone for everything that could possibly be real. However, the tide has definitely changed due simply to the sheer number of instances today. That fact is slowly changing the global understanding and view of consciousness and ourselves.

However, our current concepts of reality being what they are, the majority of the global population go from day to day never knowing or understanding the infinite things they are doing. That specifically has to do with how we affect the people around us and our moments to come with our thoughts, e-motions and physical actions. The method in which many implement the direction of life can be likened to a game of darts. One can, without looking, without forethought or focus, throw their darts in the general direction of the board. This carefree attitude of "What happens, happens!" occurs mainly because of a frustrated state from trying, while not understanding the "why" or "how" of the whole process. Then, on the other hand, there are those who try too hard, getting caught up in rituals, sabotaging their own unfolding Life moments.

By architecturally drafting your dreams and goals, then focusing on them day in and day out as you have perhaps learned to do, would be no different than an architect never showing a builder the blueprints. Once that pencil has been laid down and the blueprints are done, they must be handed over to the builder. The proper way to create dreams is to design, draw, then give them life by turning them over to the builder (the non-physical universe) to put them together. Then, you simply allow them to unfold as they should, remembering that you reflect externally that which is e-motionally within yourself.

So, let's say you have a reasonable grasp on the reality that consciousness is not dependent on the brain or body for its existence. Now, what is consciousness? Good question, but actually a rather simple one to answer. The obvious fact is that thoughts are the principal factor of what is considered consciousness. When we physically sleep, however, there is little in the way of controlled, structured thoughts. So, personal *control* or choice if you will, would also be an aspect of consciousness. So, consciousness would equal what we, in physical terms refer to as *"mind"*. I want to go a step further to answer the "from where" question by saying that "mind is the conscious, thought producing and aware state of Soul". Keep in mind that Soul is of a dimensional level prior to that of physical reality.

I want to share with you a fairly easy analogy of the non-physical transforming into physical form that I hope will stick. The importance of understanding this is that if you are to create, then you should be aware of the elements of the equation. Our analogy's starting point is going to be a sub-atomic/non-physical point where everything that is physical once began. To represent that sub-level I want you to clearly see and e-motionalize (think of at Soul level) a droplet of water. That drop of water is a representation of everything non-physical. Now allow the water drop to slowly start to fall, and just as it picks up speed it transforms to an ice crystal, becoming part of physical reality. The ice crystal represents everything that is physical in structure. The transitional point from water to ice crystal is the illustrative divide between the non-physical becoming our physical reality. Our thoughts may seemingly flow here but they traverse into what everything is made of.

Mind over Matter becomes simple, once you realize that matter has a structural foundation that is identical to mind. That is to say, mind is water just as all things physical begin. Furthermore, one in turn can affect the other. The biggest question, however is, "Which one is in control?" Is it your three-dimensional, physical world, or is it you that is mind within, pushing the internal buttons and pulling the levers of biology? Mind - is that of Soul - which is housed in biology - that exists in a three-dimensional physical reality - that is ALL made of the exact same beginnings. Remember that all the while, "E-motion" is the driving force and energy that alters the physical world, causing it to unfold into what you want or do not want.

During the portion of the holographic edification process in regard to how we design – create – and bring to Life our unfolding moments, a particular situational image was presented in the holograms. The image was one of a moment and situation in my personal life when I was fifteen. The situation ran as it should have, yet not as it actually happened. What I was shown was a scenario with no e-motional content infused. Once the image reset to its beginning point, I was instructed to direct an e-motion of choice into the situation, then allow it to unfold. The scenario then reset and I was to alter the infused e-motion again and again. As each process unfolded, the situational scenario evolved to an entirely different outcome, illustrating that the only variable is the element of e-motion. The lesson then completed.

The lesson was that within our "minds" we architecturally draft and outline what it is we want to have happen. Your thoughts of what you want, while taking place in the "mind", are flowing through the sub-level dimension from which all things come, just like a hand drawn through water. The final outcome of what we want or don't want becomes dependent upon our ability to allow moments to unfold as they should. The alternative would be to continue altering outcomes by the e-motional content we infuse into our spirit-rendered blueprints. Being aware of what is immediately to come depends upon one's ability to create and maintain an e-motional blank slate in given situations.

If we drift ever so slightly sideways, away from the discussion on consciousness and mind for a moment to take a closer look at e-motions, I believe this element shall become clear. I've used a hyphen in the word throughout the book to emphasize its foundation and characteristics. E-motions are the electrical current drawn from the non-physical by way of Soul's connection, to set in motion the physical. Their infusion into the time that is ever unfolding just ahead of us alters that unfolding. E-motions affect in a positive or negative way, depending on their polarity. That by no means is to say that what we refer to as a positive thought or e-motion carries the matching polarity. The same is also true for negative thought and e-motional input.

Can you have a positive thought coupled with a magnetically bound positive e-motion? Obviously not, as you cannot have the same poles together. Well, I guess you could duct-tape the two together, but even at that, there would still remain a gap between the two, while the physical unfolding of that situation collapses. This situation should ring a bit of a bell for the few who feel they're forever trying to push or drive a square peg through a round hole.

Once you have the electricity of an e-motion infused, you present a soft magnetic field into the mix. That then has a positive/push or negative/pull aspect to it. If you stop and really think about that for a second or two, you will understand that a negative particle anywhere in the universe is going to draw or attract its direct opposite to complete itself. E-motions such as hope, want, fear that a given situation won't happen, worry and many others will either create a monster, or push it away all together.

As the architect you are, you design with the consciousness of Soul, draft with the heart of all that you are, setting it free to the non-physical to build for you, then do the physical reality things to help bring it into the world of your Life.

CHAPTER 12

Life's GPS

*Learning to read the signposts
along the Journey...*

"Life is actually easy,
for it is us who have made it difficult."

—*Alan R. Stevenson*

Rebekah wrote in to say:

"Even in spirit, we have free will... you chose to come back and share your knowledge with everyone, good for you... I'm so grateful for that! I thought that I'd had an NDE a few years ago. It was triggered by a nasty fall face first into a gravel road... I didn't faint, it was the universe nudging me to "act". That was the beginning of my journey "into" myself, but I came through it and opened up the light within me.

Keep shining your love & light Alan."

Most of today's technologies leave a lot of us wondering how we possibly managed to get by without them. The fact is however, we did. Yet, only through the advent of technology are we more aware and realize the methods of the past were nowhere near as effective or as efficient.

The global positioning system or GPS as it is better known, isn't one of those technological advancements I use all that often. Yet, in the same breath I can say that it's one of the more significant technical improvements I appreciate today. On a warm summer's day, where the intent usually is to get lost during a long, aimless motorcycle ride, with the GPS on my cell I can find my way out in only a few moments from wherever I end up. Just like the maps in mega malls that place an "X" saying "You are here," the GPS does the exact same thing, but on a much larger scale. As I've learned, knowing where you are first, is rather important when considering where it is you want to go.

Just like you, I pretty much always got to where I needed to go prior to the GPS. That's not to say it wasn't achieved without any difficult challenges at times. Printed maps are not much help when it comes to being lost at an unnamed back roads intersection, surrounded by fields of six-foot-tall corn. Regardless of the direction you decide to go, it nearly always ends up being the wrong way. With this advancement of the GPS, embarking on a journey has become so much more simple and less worrisome.

It is not very hard to imagine how stuck you would be if you were in a foreign country without a map or a GPS and had to drive across the country. To achieve your cross-country trip, you'd start out in what you believed to be the best possible direction. Then, along the way, you'd hopefully run into people who could help guide you with directions. The task would, no doubt, prove to be challenging, yet on the day you were born, you were handed a similar task in a roundabout way. For so many people, living life with all of its intricacies today has become every bit as difficult and perhaps more complicated to navigate as the trip described above. Along the journey of life, situations arise in which we look to other people, as to the what, why and how to head in the proper direction.

Before my heart attack and NDE, I remember feeling rather lost at different points in my life. They were times of being so unsure of which way to turn in a given situation, only being sure of which direction was up or down. I was extremely lucky to have had the father I did, knowing he was always there to assist and guide me. I have learned since, by listening to, and talking with more and more people that these difficulties are a common life experience. Still, this stems back to the statement I made before, that none of us were born with a hand manual or guide to life, per se. So, wouldn't it be nice to have a hand-held GPS device to help guide us through life? (though there may currently be an app for that...)

Considering events of the past, I came to realize my course of action nearly always carried me to points and situations I didn't want to be at or in. I was constantly wondering how the heck did I end up here? Of course, you'd think after grabbing hold of the hot burner of life a few times, you would clue in, or at least switch up the methods that got you into those situations in the first place. Then, on the other end of the stick are those who carefully plan their paths and/or lives out, only to end up with something far less than their envisioned expectations. The balance point, however, is in the middle of the stick.

I'm not about to say that at times I don't find myself in moments of uncertainty, but then again, I wouldn't call it uncertainty. With the change of perception and the way in which I live my life, I see it more as learning by feeling, doing and Being.

On the day you were born you started out with a GPS instilled within you - a guidance system that helped you learn, prior to understanding language and verbal instruction. After gaining a sufficient amount of understanding and acclimating to physical life and living, we begin to let go of what got us to that point. Hence the slide from what we actually are to searching, instead, for who we are.

It is not that the instilled guidance system has been deleted from within, it has simply deteriorated to some degree due to a lack of use. As infants, we are an incredible sponge of learning, absorbing all we physically hear, see and feel. We e-motionalize at a different level: a raw state of true essence and state of Being. If you wish to understand more of the mysteries of life and living, simply watch an infant grow on a time-lapse video. It is there you will see a Soul navigate the transition back to the physical.

Some people may be thinking or feeling that I'm talking about what everyone else has already covered, and that would be intuition. But honestly, I am not discussing intuition. There's a marked difference, as reading the signposts of your life has more to do with the original, loosely-planned, Soul-evolving course of action that's desired. This is learning to e-motionalize internally at a level that allows you to feel and know you are right where you should be, as opposed to leaving things to a chaotic random state.

Where intuition differs is more about its purposeful use. Intuition itself works more as a moment-to-moment alarm system to warn us at appropriate times. It's what lets us know that this person is okay while that one isn't, or gives you the inkling about coming events, prior to getting in that car where your best friend is drunk behind the wheel. Seeing those quick-coming moments flash before you - now that's intuition. It works also to let us know of the good moments and things to come in the very short term.

I've learned to e-motionalize my coming moments from within, going with the flow without fear, knowing I can change my course of direction at will, but only if I am paying attention to the signs along the roadway to where I am actually heading. Knowing where you are today is that big X that says, "You are here." Knowing what direction you are supposed to go from there is your GPS. You then need only to become aware in a way you never have of the signposts along the roadway of the journey of your life.

CHAPTER 13

Seeing the Future From Here Quantum Growth...

"It is from within ourselves that we ignite the magic each day holds, though the how and why is seldom considered or understood."

—Alan R. Stevenson

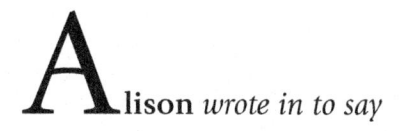

Alison *wrote in to say*

"I too have had an experience similar to yours, I was 20 and pregnant with my first son and I became extremely ill with a kidney problem. Whilst in bed waiting for the ambulance to take me to the hospital, the room became bathed in a beautiful white light. I know this sounds weird but I could actually feel the light's energy. At the end of the bed stood three figures, 2 in dazzling white suits. I could not tell whether they were men or women, but they had the most beautiful faces I have ever seen. The third person stood in the middle of them, he was dressed in a suit and looked like you or I. I was extremely frightened and said "I don't want to go!" The third figure replied "We *have not come for you, but to tell you , you have a job to do on earth and it is not your time." I spent several days in the hospital hoovering between life and death. When I returned home I told my husband and he went white. I had described the third figure and it was his father who had died years before I married him. I was shocked but over the years I have taken comfort in those angels' words."*

There have been many statements made in regard to seeing or knowing the future. Statements such as *"I should have seen that one coming.", "If only I knew before hand, I wouldn't have done that.", "If I knew then what I know now..."* and one of my favorites, not that it's one I use, however I do find it amusing: *"If I could only go back to being twenty again and start over with what I know now!"* Many of these statements show a conscious belief that if we knew what the future holds, we would be happier, safer, smarter, and more relaxed. We imagine being so relaxed that, while reading the newspaper, you'd be able to merely stretch out an arm and snag that ball flying by right out of the air, without looking at it. Wouldn't life just be grand? Perhaps it may happen in a distant time to come, but I don't see it happening any time soon, since the human race has a long road ahead of it to just comprehending what it would take to do that.

Having experienced both states of our conscious Being and existence, I have learned an important truth. You don't see near-future coming events so much as you feel them. Keep in mind that we e-motionalize at our Soul's core first, then physically feel the effects, or biological response to that infused energy.

For example, an individual passed away from within the circle of people I currently know, but it happened a few years prior to my meeting them. In a conversation about his passing, I was told he made a point of saying good-bye to his wife that morning prior to heading to work. He also made an unusual early morning trip back into the house to see his children and say good-bye as well. He knew or felt something was different, though perhaps vague, prompting him to do so. Also, my great-grandmother, who passed away at ninety-nine years of age, was one for always saying good-night before bed. My great-Aunt Beth, who looked after Grandma Thornburn for many years, told us later that Grandma had said good-bye the night she passed peacefully in her sleep. Perhaps she sensed the change in physical reality and life around her.

Though these examples may represent the extreme aspects of life and death, they more importantly show that we sense, or feel things to come. Some people are much more adept at this than others, but it's an ability we all share. Even more important, however is what it's going to take to get the body that is the Human Race to evolve in more of a "quantum leap" fashion. A need to do so is currently evident and, I might add, quite important.

For a moment, let's revisit one of those earlier statements, but more in regard to this quantum learning: *"If only I knew then what I know now."* To me, this one has always seemed to be more of an unfortunate, regretful statement, indicative of the person's life having ended up being less than it should have been. In essence, it says that if the speaker had been smarter at an earlier age, he or she wouldn't be where they are today.

Perhaps at some point you've stopped for a moment in somewhat of a daydream state, to wonder what it might be like to go tell your younger self something important that you just learned. You wanted to do so because you knew it would have made a big impact on your life at an earlier time. We may not have the ability to go back in time to do that, however we do have the ability to make a huge difference in the future of the over-all Human Race.

Is there a means by which to look down the road into the future? The answer is fundamentally dependent upon the perspective. Is it from an individual perspective, or that of the Human Race as a single unit? The variance between the two becomes "the road not taken" that Robert Frost so eloquently wrote of. We need to begin to think more as to the whole, rather then on an individual basis. We can do this by properly handing the raw essence of what we have learned backward in time to those younger than ourselves.

When a twenty-five-year-old individual stands before a person that's fifty, he or she is peering a full lifetime into the future. By the same token, the older person is peering back in time at themselves. Think of it for a moment; a twenty-five-year-old person is instilled with all that a fifty-year-old knows, down to the essence of experience. By the time that twenty-five-year-old is fifty, how much more intellectually advanced will they be than the original fifty- year-old? Done over two generations, an exponential factor comes into play.

Though a more mature example is used, a fifteen-year-old person has something to share or teach a ten-year-old. By handing back, not so much our knowledge, but more the essence of experiences and lessons learned, we bring about a new way to foster a proper growth rate, instead of a repeated pattern.

Time's elusive illusion is not something I can verbally or literally explain as I experienced it. Suffice it to say, I am pretty sure you have at one time or another had the distinct sense of the oddity of a moment you've experienced yourself. We see and feel time's illusion most drastically as we age, through the sheer speed at which a year passes by. To a four-year-old, a year would represent one quarter or 25% of that individuals life, seemingly lasting for ever. A ten-year-old sees it as 1/10. A twenty-five-year-old experiences a year as a mere $1/25^{th}$ of their life's experience, while a seventy-year-old individual feels the exponential speed of a year as a blistering $1/70^{th}$ of their journey. To learn what is needed, we must first understand that time is as much as or more of an illusion than physical reality.

The edification process I experienced with the four Beings, who, I might add, were considerably older than I, prompted me to explain an important concept and process we must learn. From the youngest to the oldest, there is no difference other than a magical one.

CHAPTER 14

Of the Heart
From the Heart

*"It is the Love from your true essence of Being,
and not the heart
that can heal any heart."*

—Alan R Stevenson

Anonymous

"Why are we (mankind) so afraid to admit we are ill?"

Though the statistics on heart attacks were mentioned earlier in the book, I've added this chapter for a whole host of reasons. For one, I'm not only an NDE experiencer, more importantly I am, first and foremost, a heart attack survivor. If we consider *cause & effect* for a moment, where the heart attack was the cause of my NDE, then the heart attack should carry a greater precedence. The NDE clearly was an interesting, consciousness expanding, warm, loving experience, yet heart attack information doesn't carry the same warm, fuzzy disposition.

Therefore, it isn't sought after with nearly the same vigor as the search by individuals for spiritual understanding.

To refresh the incredible odds against so many human beings today, lets take a closer second look, shall we? While looking for figures to back up my numbers, I found that the CDC has a set of numbers, while another document had other figures, and four others had a different set of numbers all together. I was left with the feeling that there must be different concepts, ideas and formulas at work here. That being the case, I decided to go with what my original cardiologist told me.

It wasn't until my first stress test that I met the doctor who would become my regular cardiologist. Due to the severe biological nature of the heart attack, my doctor entered me into a five-year global study, collecting data for research purposes. When I asked him why I was being put into the study, he told me that 87% of survivors do not survive another five years post-initial heart attack. Not exactly the kind of news you want to hear only a few weeks after such an experience. It was hoped that the data collecting would give them a better understanding as to why the stats are so poor. Unfortunately, within that first year I moved a fair distance away to attend school, and had to leave the study. As of this writing I am heading into my sixth post-heart attack year.

The number one spot on the top ten list of causes of death, year in and year out, has been and will continue to be related to heart disease. It has held the position since as far back as 1914 through, as far as I can tell, 2014. During that hundred-year stretch, medical advancements as well as many others, such as vehicles and organized response teams, have eliminated most causes from the list. Although the face of that list has changed, the exception is still the number one spot. Having experienced a major heart attack for a three-day duration makes me somewhat more of an expert to tell you why, than the experts. I, for one, when planning a trip, would rather talk to someone who's been to a certain destination, as opposed to someone who has merely read about it. Please remember, although we're talking just about heart disease, this is by no means meant to minimize the importance of, or demean the multitudes of individuals who have passed on by way of, any of the other nine on that list.

You may recall my earlier statement that roughly only eight out of one-hundred heart attack victims survive the initial experience. That in itself makes it somewhat difficult to take when you think that ninety-two human Souls didn't have a chance the moment their heart attack started - or did they? This is a question we will perhaps try to answer.

If we use these same stats, for every one-hundred heart attack survivors, a total of about 1,300 heart attacks would have happened. Focusing a bit more on the small group of one hundred survivors paints a dismal picture as we track them through a short period of time. Only five years hence, of the original 1,300 heart attacks and one hundred survivors, there remain a mere 13 individuals, of which I am one.

There are a few eye-opening truths for women to digest and come to terms with. Heart disease is by far the number one killer of women, though you may have thought it to be something else. The staggering fact is that H.D. is many times deadlier than all cancers combined. Breast cancer has received so much attention in recent years that it is at the forefront of most women's minds. Rest assured, I'm not trying to detract from those with breast cancer, as I also have a dearly loved family member who is a breast cancer survivor. The thing about cancer is that it is something we feel with everything that we are at the core of our Being as it slowly sucks the life out of a loved one. That's not to mention that it does the same to the pockets of an entire family. We unfortunately witness it in a near-slow-motion sense. On the other hand, in most cases of heart attacks, it is as though someone stepped up beside you and turned out the Light that is you. Heart attacks come quickly, often with misunderstood cues or little to no symptoms and then a loved one is gone.

The fact remains that, while 1 in 31 American women die from breast cancer each year, it is a 1 in only 3 factor when it comes to heart disease and women. Furthermore, this gender-owned disease concept is about as silly as most of the antics that go on in preschool sandboxes. Just as osteoporosis was thought to be a woman's disease, only around 54% of cases are women. Since 1984 though, more women die each year from heart attacks than men. So - the raw truth? You are ten times more likely to have a heart attack than any other thing. So perhaps it is time for you to redirect your attention and plan of action in regard to your health status. Now, just because your mother and/or grandmother died of a heart attack does not, and I repeat DOES NOT mean that you have to have one or will have one.

To come to understand why the current statistics are so poor, though, a simple question needs to be asked. "How does an individual go from being an entity in peak health to one having a heart attack?" Further understanding is acquired by acknowledging the fact that it's a process and not just something that happens out of thin air. So many talk about it being more about genetics, which, from my personal point of view, is turning a blind eye to the actual cause. It is more about what we do to our physical vehicle/body, than it is about anything else. People have a tendency to look after their car in the driveway better than they do themselves. Common sense seemingly illustrates a clear picture when Grandpa and Dad have already stepped to the other side via a heart attack, that John Jr. will as well, but that's so far from the actual truth! The absolute only thing common to those three is... you guessed it, their diet.

The second factor of this process we are taking a look at is that human biology is alkaline by natural state of being, yet is acid by it's function. In that fact lies the greatest head-scratching contradiction going. By way of a cell's own functions it creates its very own destruction and demise. Acids must be neutralized and by-products or remnants should be rinsed away with an alkaline solution to create a neutral environment for cells to complete their proper mitosis cycles. I remember a scene in the movie *The Lion King* in which Simba steps up on Pride Rock to take over, and the rains pour down, washing away all the old, for the new to begin. The environment in which the birth of a new cell takes place determines the cell's vitality. The environment of a cell means everything, just as Dr.

Bruce Lipton has pointed out in his books, based on his studies and knowledge.

What's this got to do with heart disease and heart attacks? Once you stop and think about what acid will do to your skin if it sits on it for any length of time, you'll have a better understanding. Yes, it burns, but more importantly, the acid drys your skin out and then it cracks. What do we do with cracks on the surface of our skin? We put ointment on and then seal them so that they can heal properly. Your internal mechanisms do the exact same thing when it comes to internal cracks. Every time your heart beats it puts an extreme amount of stress on the plumbing directly attached to it. Now, if you add mildly acidic blood flowing through the heart for, say, twenty or thirty years, that plumbing becomes dry, brittle and more ridged than it once was. Those mechanisms go about filling the cracks with a very sticky substance. At that point, the substances we ingest have the perfect primer coat to adhere to just as paint sticks to its primer base coat. Particles of these ingested, mildly sticky substances get into our bloodstreams and slowly build up at those patched areas. Over time the arteries become blocked. Pressure builds up behind the blockage just like a pinched off garden hose, causing further arterial damage. As I said earlier, it's a process.

I don't want to point anyone in a given direction as it would be far better for you to do your own research, considering I am not a doctor. Your doctor should be one of your best friends, in that you can tell them anything, rather than fear going to see them. Keep in mind that there are several different types of doctor just as there are people, because doctors are people too. There are those that just write scripts, and don't know you at all, then there are those well-rounded ones. Doctors, however, are not always the end-all-to-be-all. In fact, it is you, yourself that is, with the decisions you make and choices you follow through with. If your doctor listens to you, guides and assists you with practical methods to maintain or obtain your desired health, he or she is a keeper.

Statistics are merely numbers and not a narrow pathway you are doomed to walk down as you age. Though it can be a bit overwhelming to sort through so much misinformation for good information, I encourage you to at least consider it. By way of a balanced biological vehicle as opposed to swinging extremes of health status, we are afforded the opportunity to experience, learn, grow and evolve at the important soul and spiritual level. Life was meant to be, just as you are here and now. Cherish it with a healthy, open heart and mind.

CHAPTER 15

The Inescapable

"It is through true understanding of the truth that we all become capable."

—Alan R. Stevenson

Paula *wrote in to say;*

"Why is it that once we are faced with death we don't fear it, we feel peace instead? Is it because we accept it, or because at that moment we remember who we truly are? I once believed I was going to die. I was 14 and foolishly jumped in the deep end of a swimming pool and didn't know how to swim. Never been in a swimming pool before. My body went straight down towards the bottom. In a split second I realized what I did, and the only thought was "I am going to die", no fear just a feeling of acceptance and peace. I really did believe that "this is it." It felt like so much time had elapsed when in reality must have been seconds. Two lifeguards came to my rescue and pulled me out.

Thank you for sharing Alan. Death is not to be feared I guess."

Namaste

Prior to our own day of shedding the glove of our physical body, we first must come to understand the transitions of those we've loved and cherished. While their passing is actually supposed to help us in regard to our own day to come, it's developed into something completely different. The process of physical life sets up a path of perception we can't help but have. An emptiness created by a loved one's departure affirms the perception within ourselves, further fostering the belief in the finality of death and their passing. As we tie the emotional and mental aspects to the physicality of their passing, there's a sense of knowing we'll be with them again. This knowing is typically mistaken for the hope and longing to be with them. Some have said this is merely an emotional coping mechanism that only settles in after we've become tired of the unsettling internal conflict. It is a struggle forged by the frantic searching through the helplessness within ourselves for answers and some kind of understanding toward what we think of as closure.

At times like these, many individuals become hopelessly lost. The emptiness we feel is because we do not know where the personality or essence of the person we loved and knew has gone. Are they really, truly and honestly gone for good? How can that be? It isn't possible! Our beliefs, concepts and inability to perceive the truth tell us, "Yes," while our Soul knows better and fights to piece things together. Unfortunately, the bond that unequivocally holds each of us together also creates the quicksand of life when a loved one is lost. Missing a person that's transitioned on presents moments of feeling helpless, which can add to our exhausting search for an understanding that is sorely needed. Once we are emotionally, mentally and physically drained, a state of desolation emerges that only the act of making a choice and the passage of time can heal.

It is devastating to see an individual become so paralyzed within his or her own life due to the passing of a loved one. They become trapped in the situation, which doesn't allow them to proceed on with life as it was meant to be. For those I've helped escape the quicksand, it was done by simply showing them that their mental and emotional state created what is known as a magnetic lock. They come to understand that the combination of the two internal states of emotion and thoughts magnetically stick them to the physical occurrence of a loved one's passing. Then, there are those who are carrying an unnecessary burden around in silence over a loved one's passing. These burdens come in many different emotional forms, with guilt being the most prominent one for many. The one truth I would like you to understand about the burden those people carry is, if it was actually important to your life's purpose or the passed person's life, then they'd still be here to complete it.

It is perhaps possible that you, just as I have several times during my life, asked the question, "What is it like to die?" As a young boy, what normally followed for me was a deep sadness. Then, the internal statement nearly always came rushing forth, "I don't want to die! I never want to die!" Though a five or six year old is still fairly close to the actual process, they, in the physical sense, don't truly understand the biological process involved. Later, as adults, because of what we've witnessed and learned, we're forced into coming to grips with our own mortality. As regrettable as it may be, far too many have the perception *"It is what it is; end of story!"* I am back again and here now to tell you that it ISN'T, nor could it possibly be any further from the truth! It is through true understanding of the truth that we all become capable.

I'm here to tell you that everything your life has given you the ability to see and understand is but a mere fraction of the circle of life. Unfortunately, our current concept of that circle of life is still only half complete. For most people, this concept places birth and death at 12 o'clock on that circle. This concept leaves a gap in the circle, detaching it and equating to more of an arc. Our linear thinking and understanding makes it easy to roll out this line, giving it the beginning and end, as we currently, but unfortunately view life. And you know what? I get it! The intangible blank spot of that second half is like swiping your hand at thin air to come up with a handful of very little, from a physical perspective.

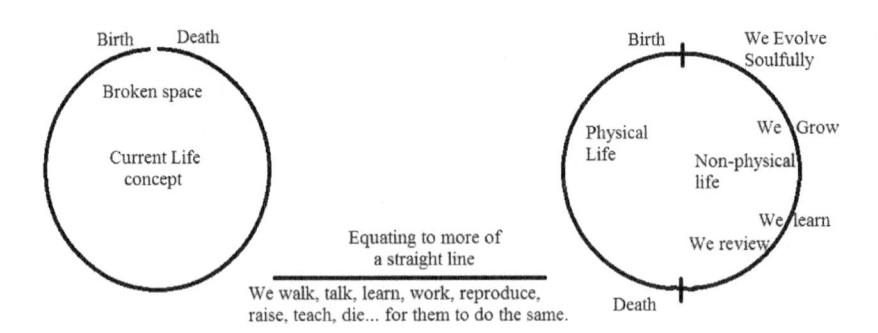

Left circle: Birth, Death, Broken space, Current Life concept. Equating to more of a straight line. We walk, talk, learn, work, reproduce, raise, teach, die... for them to do the same.

Right circle: Birth, We Evolve Soulfully, Physical Life, We Grow, Non-physical life, We learn, We review, Death.

Why can't we remember our non-physical existence? At the end of our physical lives, most of the data of our memories is lost to our physical perception, due to data dumping. Imagine trying to carry all that in-between life data around with you.

Beginning a new life would become so burdened with those memories, the purpose of your physical existence would be compromised. If you think of your current life's available memory storage as a computer thumb drive, you should get the idea. Nothing, and I do mean nothing you've ever thought, felt or done is lost, as it all becomes a part of the non-physical thought and image form. Hence, our responsibility to our thoughts, feelings and actions during life - not only because they create our moments to come, but ultimately the path the Being you are follows.

Death isn't some thin dude in a bad piece of fashion, carrying an antique farm implement. No Being comes to suck the life force and energy out of your physical body, leaving a corn husk behind for someone to dispose of. However, you can see how it does illustrate the many outdated and antiquated beliefs that still exist in our modern society. Our loved one's passing as well as our own is more of what Paula mentioned when she wrote a comment to me. She really did state it correctly by saying "Death is not to be feared I guess!" Though there still is some uncertainty in her statement, death truly isn't to be feared, as fear alters the way in which we live - or don't live - our lives!

"Why must we die at all?" On one hand, we never really do in the most important way, yet on the other hand, our physical self's days are numbered. On the surface, we understand just by the premise of physical biology's function that it can't last forever. That is, however, merely a factor of the grand plan, which pertains to the purpose of life. Reid Tracey of HayHouse recently wrote that his son taught him an important acronym, YOLO, meaning "You only live once." Although correct and true in terms of who you currently, physically are, it is not true as to what you are always.

Once the electrical Soul Being we are is in distress of one form or another, be it disease, aging or an accident, many comforting perceptibility factors come into play. It is here we come to understand the truth about time and finally realize that it doesn't exist as it seems to stop. During the physical process of transitioning on, we uncouple, in a way, from physical reality, while we are still a part of our physical bodies. This is where the Soul that you are redirects e-motional attachment from the physical to the non-physical point of origin. In doing so, the only real e-motion that exists on the other side, which is a peaceful, serene, loving calm, is remembered. Once settled to this state, we gravitate toward it and away from our bodies. What we can perceive and understand by the things or people we already know in a physical sense aids us. This is a great comforting spot for us to be in during this unfamiliar time of transition. The forms your guides and teachers can take will have much more to do with your true e-motionally connected ties prior to heading homeward.

Windows & designed time-lines for Soul evolution...

Jim *wrote in to say;*

"Alan, interesting indeed. I have had three occasions where I knew in advance that I was in great danger (life ending danger). I don't know how I knew, I just did. I took action (including telling *somebody) on each occasion and in 2 of the 3 times those actions resulted in me still being alive. The one time I acted differently than I normally would, I got blown up by a mine in Vietnam. I suppose that I was lucky to be only wounded instead of killed — it could have gone either way. Something strange goes on around us in this life. I do not claim to understand it, but I have definitely seen it (3 times)."*

We each have close calls and near misses during our lives that we call brushes with death. We are never really aware of most of these situations when they happen. There are, however, those few that force us to wipe our brow when realizing just how lucky we were at that moment. All of these near brushes with death are what is known as functional windows of Soul evolution. At the onset of life, there exists a desired goal and an unimaginable combination of factors for that objective to take place. A Soul only ever returns home when it is supposed to, prioritized only by its need to evolve in a given direction first and foremost. At birth, there's a flexing situational time-line. Though not written in stone, it is, however the needed direction to evolve. This becomes the purpose for this life, here and now. If you were to have a list of important things you wished to learn, then prioritized the process to do so, you'd have an organized plan. Each Soul has an unwritten list to work on, for which a plan is created, driven by the Soul's desire to evolve to its greatest potential.

Let's say that during this life, your required lessons for desired Soul evolution had to do with confidence of your self worth. To simplify things, we'll use the analogy of a hallway or corridor as your life's time-line for clarity of explanation. Upon being born, you'd be at one end of this very long hallway, unable to see the other end. At the point of birth, you only need to walk that corridor and step through a door at the other end. That door represents the end of a physical life and is a direct link to another life in a sequence related to the current life's plan. Along the corridor, however, there are a few other doors. These are the windows of opportunity for the Soul to go in another direction, should the elements of this life not unfold as originally planned. As we pass these doors on our timeline, brushes with death occur. The multitude of factors of the original plan that must come together are, at the least shall we say, very extreme. Should they not do so, the originally planned corridor of your life begins to dissolve from its end back toward current time. At that point, available windows to other potential scenarios of evolution begin to open and you step through. These new doors and the originally planned one are not linked in any way and a whole new path has begun.

While writing this chapter, I was told that I am glorifying death, or at least it surely seemed like it. I can assure you that is not my intent whatsoever. I responded to the statement by merely saying the thoughts and perceptions of a destination you have while planning a holiday are never totally congruent with the experience of that destination. Hence, my perspective of Being here and Life itself have drastically changed. The concept is, perhaps, very alien to those around me, at times creating a difficult challenge.

We do, however, need to stop separating the Soul as a secondary component, setting it on a shelf out of the way. Though our physical body is, for the most part, who we have become, we must stop idolizing the physical body as *what* we are. Take the non-physical, electrical current of the Soul Being you truly are out of biology, and what is it that you have?

My truest and deepest wish for you is to understand both halves of the circle of life, ultimately altering your fear and the way in which you live your life to its highest and greatest purpose.

CHAPTER 16

Walking the Journey

> "That which is rigid flowing down the rocky rapids of life gets broken upon the rocks, yet what remains flexible floats with and upon the water."
>
> —Alan R. Stevenson

Shelley wrote in to say;

Thank you. I have been studying and reading about NDE's for the last 20 years, before it became so mainstream. My first introduction was thru Helen Kubler Ross and then Raymond Moody. Being a nurse I saw and "felt" things with dying patients that I couldn't explain. 20 years ago to talk of any of this stuff was to be ridiculed. So grateful that the "veil" is lifting and people are being exposed to this new reality. I look forward to reading your book and will keep searching and seeking as I always have.

Blessings dear one

It is a long road we wander
As we walk we ponder

> Looking always back
> then ahead yonder
>
> For time's illusion
> Is but all we squander
>
> Yet know there is
> no other step
> Of which you should be fonder
>
> Than this one now...
>
> —*Alan R. Stevenson*

From the moment we are conceived, intellectually and emotionally by two Beings who come to understand the true essence of what Love really is, our journey into physical life begins. During our physical life path we forget that state of origin, by way of adopting means to define our physical life and who we are within it, unaware that those means also confine what we are. As of the time of birth, we learn from those who precede our footsteps as to what to do and how along the journey of life. We are taught the same methods they were taught, creating a repetitious state of Being. It isn't until we, ourselves become parents that we're reminded of the true core emotion, through the connection and Love of a child, which we have seemingly forgotten.

While walking our journey of physical life, we stumble from time to time or perhaps even fall down, stopping to analyze and wonder what it was we stumbled on. We sift through the aspects of a given situation to try and learn from them. The life path I was walking prior to that fate-filled day was conceived out of what I'd learned and believed was the way in which life was meant to be. In the fall of 09' the journey became more of a "being led down the garden path" by my beliefs and thoughts of those beliefs. That process created a pinball game scenario that flashed "TILT" on the very screen of my life. Then, with no operational targeted objectives, bumpers, or manual deflecting paddles, my slow-rolling decent gained momentum. Having no reference point with which to garner any kind of clear understanding, life rolled onward toward the hole my shiny sphere was to drop through on February 26, 2010. Leading up to that day, I felt the oddity that life had taken on, and I knew it, yet with no parameters from which to gauge, I didn't understand what was happening. Ultimately, this created an absolute, definitive point of being lost, physically, emotionally and mentally. The totality of the trauma and drama of that day was simply because I didn't get it!

Today, there are far too many cells of the Human Race in the exact same situation - lost in the truest sense of the word. It doesn't matter from which culture or location on the planet, it remains the same. Though the point of an individual's perspective may be slightly altered due to those factors, the true value of a individual Being is lost to the whole when in that state. Once the individual Being's purpose is considered, their true value to the whole is properly understood. Therein, the purpose of life is one of the important common bonds we all share.

A quote from a recent Indie film entitled, *"Mistress America"* exemplifies that raw sense of being lost, and is a sentiment I believe too many feel today. A character in the film states "I am just in love with everything, but can't figure out how to make myself work in this world." Making ourselves work within this physical journey becomes a means to an end. We all seem to have the know-how; unfortunately the answers are always just out in front of us in space and time, and we are unable to grasp them with the total clarity we desire. A day arrives when the path narrows and then ends before we fully comprehend our true purpose and reason for Being.

Over the course of our lives, each of us becomes what could be considered life mechanics just like an auto mechanic is to a car, but in regard to life itself. There's no shop manual in its true sense to reference when the need may arise. There's also little in the way of proper training at the beginning of our journey, with a course curriculum more indicative of a blind apprenticeship. Through recursive physical life lessons we try to learn about life on the fly only by way of what we've seen, experienced, e-motionalized and physically felt. Then, there is also what we've been told by others of the how to do. They too, however have merely come to a point of perception and belief by the very same method. We become these mechanics, of and to our lives in an attempt to fix something for which we have but only subtle clues as to the cause of our challenges and problems. However, we do see, feel and experience the ever-so-obvious manifestation of their effects.

Just like the automotive mechanic who strips apart a motor to see and hopefully understand why it doesn't run well or work at all, we do the very same with our lives. Once taken apart and even after every valuable component has been tested, there remains nothing visually obvious to aid in solving the problem. The mechanic then goes about putting the entire motor back together, only to have it not work at all. So begins the revolving process once again of tear it down, strip it apart, examine thoroughly and analyze, then put it all back together again.

You will undoubtedly continue to jump from lily-pad to lily-pad in an effort to search for a way to fix your life, until you are shown exactly what it is you are and how that governs your stay here in this physical realm.

Physical life situations seemingly create a need for more energy at times. Being continuously soft-wired to our dimension of origin, from which the Soul draws its sustaining energy, creates a bit of a problem at times. The unfortunate aspect of that fact is that we have a tendency in given situations to, in a defensive manner, rotate our dial of electrical flow to full-on. That internal dial acts just like a dimmer switch in a roundabout way, for our e-motions, which allows less or more current to flow. If your mind's visual acuity is clear in regard to your soft-wired connection, you will perhaps never look at a streetcar connected to overhead electrical lines in the same way ever again! With that internal dial turned to full on, however, though unaware of what we're doing, we draw 15 to 20 times the required flow needed to cope with and handle specific situations. Once a physical situation is initiated, then thought and e-motionalized by you, that energy must go somewhere. Similar to a light bulb or computer CPU that has too much electricity flowing through it, it pops a circuit or blows entirely! Most people have either experienced this situation and process, or at least witnessed an individual who has literally vibrated internally and externally from excessive draw of Life force. That Life-Force is the sub-level electrical flow that is life, existence, awareness, and the Loving God source. No one in their right mind would walk over to a downed power line and pick it up just to see what would happen, yet we pretty much do the same thing with our e-motions in a free play game mode day in and day out.

As I learned the hard way, the base factor while you walk the journey is how we are with ourselves first and foremost, affecting how we interact with others we meet along the way. How you come to e-motionalize, think of and then feel physically toward yourself has everything to do with the proper understanding, or lack of understanding about the Being you are. This either allows for, or doesn't allow the true spirit connection that so many seek. It is through a learned peacefulness, however that we become balanced enough to further learn how to control our flow of electricity/life source and the resulting magnetic field, so as not to affect those around us and not to be affected by them.

Bowling balls, pins and balloons...

Personalities are a reaction to the draw of energy from its origin which directly influences our magnetic field. An individual's personality is a reflection of their magnetic field and vice-versa. The energy a person draws from source of origin creates within the Soul a specific e-motionalization of that energy, then presents it as a certain magnetic field. That magnetic field is proportionate to the personality we see, e-motionalize and feel from another human Being. This is evidenced by witnessing the changing of that personality. For the most part, we sense the state of Being in the people we know, long before physically or verbally interacting with them.

We've all seen and dealt with or been affected by a bowling ball-type personality at one time or another. These Souls have merely adopted beliefs and perspectives based on their physical life experiences, developing a mindset that must be of a certain manner to achieve a specific outcome in a situation, or their lives as a whole. The individual draws high energy while pulling hard from the source of origin in a continual, forceful manner. As I said before, that energy MUST go somewhere, resulting in an highly ridged and influencing magnetic field. Two "bowling ball" magnetic fields together will invariably make for a lot of clanking and sparks, of no benefit to anyone.

Bowling pins, on the other hand, have a narrowly ridged and often defensive magnetic field, held close and fairly tight unto themselves. They are, however too thinly balanced, toppling at times to mere slight gusts of wind, or perhaps I should say life situations. These Souls can become stuck in physical life situations by unreasonable fears. Fear is an e-motion of a set frequency which disrupts and to a degree distorts an individual's magnetic field. The energy they draw can be likened to a foot full on the gas pedal, then totally off again, repeatedly. Their search for true balance during their journeys evolves more into a frustrated state of Being. Yet they, too, can find the peacefulness within by letting go and allowing for a more flexible state, once they understand that it will not and cannot harm them. For them, learning that, however, can be a challenge.

Balloon-type magnetic fields that range from being somewhat firm to flexible enough with others to present more of a self-protective stance than a defensive one. They can scale down to a soft, billowing magnetic field, similar to that of the Earth, which gently flows with the solar winds. These personality types can allow others into their field as they choose to, or participate with someone or in a given situation without being affected at an emotional Soul level by adverse outcomes. Some balloons find the peacefulness of the full range while others stick to one of the various degrees.

The most prominent method of interaction by the cells of the Human Race has been the electronic connective tissue of the Internet. It has created a beginning point for those individual cells to come together. It has, however, become less useful of late in this role, and more destructive instead. Fortunately, you do have a choice to participate or not. Once we learn to show what we are through the Love that we are, it will once again provide the connectivity it originally did.

Some other challenges we face during our journeys of life are due to the continual need to force the miraculous nature of your infinite essence into a small, sociologically constructed box. The one thing that never ceases to amaze me, is how the small box builders always seem to end up on the outside of their constructions. Obviously, to be truly balanced we must learn when and how to be what we are, while considering individual situations and circumstances and avoiding the prior cranking of that internal rheostat to full-on. Always remember that the fuel that runs the GPS that will guide you is the Love you originated in, come from, and at a point will return to.

Dot-to-dot connecting.

In order to connect all the dots in the best comprehensible sequence, we must first find the starting point or dot from which to begin. During the holographic edification process, the dots, though connected, were broken up by examples from personal physical life experiences for clarification. This venue of the book doesn't allow for all the finer details of examples for each dot. Therefore, it is wished that you search your own personal life experience to clarify some or all of the dots. In doing so, your personal points of reference should better serve your own, individual understanding. If the Beings of 111 had shown me another individual's life experiences instead of my own, it is possible that I may not have understood the lessons of the dot connecting as well as I did. The same is wished for you so that you may come to that point of clarity.

Think of the overall picture as a fair-sized cube, constructed of individual square *Lego* pieces, where each piece represents one of the dots. The cube represents You, your Life and the physical world it is played out upon, which could not exist without its components.

So, let's walk slowly, shall we, while piecing together the important dots and elements. The beginning point must be our original state of consciousness and Being, which is that of the initial sub-level point that everything physical is made of. This would be considered stepping back prior to the formation of the atom. The further back you go, the deeper dimensional shifting, or phasing you will be doing. If you fan the pages of this book from the last page to the first page, the book itself represents physical reality wherein the first page is the deepest dimensional phase, long before the atom's structural formation.

Now, the components of the atom have a sub-level as just mentioned, however once joined together to construct the atom, a new, atomic dimensional level is created. The electron is the stabilizing component that allows the atom's existence. Because of the charge of the electron, a soft magnetic field is and must be present. That magnetic field has positive and negative aspects, or more important for illustrative purposes, aspects of repulsion and attraction to it. Those "push and pull" factors affect us every day of our lives.

As for physical life, each of us comes to this physical realm by choice, to improve our understanding and existence as an ethereal Being. The choice to do so becomes the purpose of physical Life. The Soul Being we are integrates with the biology of who we are at biology's sub-level, foundation point. This point is equal to Soul, or better put, if we reverse engineer biology back to its sub-atomic levels, we get to a point that is equal to or is the same as Soul.

The Soul is continuously wired to the source of origin through the non-physical capacitors, which act as electrical distribution centers, known as chakras. Soul never needs recharging, yet the biology of who you are does, as it depletes quickly. Think of biology as a battery on a slow trickle charge. Once the physical body is active in one or more ways, the slow charge is outpaced to the point of depletion. In case you didn't already know, a battery without proper water levels doesn't charge very well, or not at all. Physical biology acts in the same manner, along with the water providing clear highways for electrically based cell communication.

With our essence being comprised of electricity, we possess a soft magnetic field and our e-motions directly affect the frequency and amplitude of that field. Our e-motions are the key secret to the type of life we give to the moments and situations that unfold in front of us.

With our thoughts also being of an electrical nature and of a sub-set that flows through the dimension from the origin of all things physical, coupled with emotional input, our moments come to life. I wish for you to seriously consider the simple fact that the negative side of a magnet draws to, or attracts, while the positive end repels or pushes away. Thoughts, e-motions, actions! So it is our thoughts that architecturally draft the moments of our lives, while the sub-level universe goes about constructing those moments we desire. However it is the polarity of our e-motional content that creates the situations and circumstances of a push away or pull to us state. So the moments and situations you are in were created by you, either by forethought or by unconscious auto-default mode by way of your mere existence.

I fully admit that if the events of February 26th 2010 had not taken place, my life would perhaps still be on a dead track to an end, if not already over. The extreme course correction of my life by way of the effort and Love shown by Tiger and the Beings of 111 made me realize I was worthy of that effort and Love. It's a gift we're all given and one we can share if we properly choose to. Even when the e-motionalized events of your day might impede your desire to do so, your reward for stepping forth and beyond those events may create a small, yet important course correction that is amazing. Having been at the point I was, then progressing to where I ended up and on to the point to which I've come, I can honestly say there's little if anything more wondrous than that which you are, here and now.

I assure you, only the physical Life we live has a beginning and an end. What we are is and shall always be, regardless of the appearance of a birth and death cycle. There is simply a transition in which everything you are and have become during your Life merely slides effortlessly and painlessly from this world, back to our place of origin. How we walk that physical corridor of Life while we're here is a journey that's just as varied as the current population of this planet we call home. Though we share a unique difference in physical Life as well as non-physical existence, we all have the origin of our essence as a common bond. There is a point of origin, or place if you will, that knows only the Love that created it, which more individuals each day come to know and refer to as the God-Source.

The only true, God-given right you've always had since the moment your essence became aware, was to be what your initial awareness afforded you the potential to become and were meant to be. Even though the aspects of appearance and perception of physical life diminish your realization of your potential, they can never truly harm it, as it will always remain intact. The fact that you were aware yesterday, you are today and will be tomorrow is evidence that protects your unique potential. It is for you to merely become peaceful enough at your core, or heart of the Soul you are to discover it. Then, to shine as big and bright as the stars in the cosmos, you need only to give it life. Science says your physical essence was created by the dust of stars, and I know that your essence of Being is enough to ignite that star. To create that star, you must e-motionalize it, then physically feel it, by way of stretching out from your essence of Soul. That Soul Being is electrical and *what you are*, and have always been, long before you became *who you are* now.

CHAPTER 17

Messages from 111

"An empty hand is never truly empty for it holds within it a point of the multidimensional universe that is connected to the rest of its vast entirety"

—Alan R. Stevenson

Lori wrote in to say;

"Just wanted to Thank You - My brother recently passed and before he did he kept mentioning people in his ICU room. There was no one there but us - but he insisted there were three men there. Now after reading your story I feel a sense of calmness that he is okay and someone was there to meet him... The number three seems interesting to me...

Thanks for sharing your story - So well written and inspiring"

There were four other entities of consciousness present on the doorstep of heaven during my NDE on that day. There were three Beings I've referred to as the Teacher and the students, as well as Tiger, the facilitator. All four Beings have been known to many through the ages as angels and to this, I wholeheartedly, with all that I am, agree. My NDE by way of the Loving care of those four Beings provided me with the opportunity to understand how this trick or illusion of physical life has come about and is done.

There was nothing in my life prior to that day to help prepare my ability to comprehend the whole experience. By the same token, there is more than likely nothing in your physical life that could aid you as well, unless you've experienced it for yourself. I could string as many beautiful words as I like together in a lyrical description and still end up far from the intended objective, paled only by the vain attempt. I know, however, that it is there and where it is, because I now know of the Love I am of and the Love I am from. Within that, I stepped into a new groove of perception and understanding upon returning to a new start. I also got my chance to start over with all I had learned and known prior to the experience.

These messages, during the hard times of doing the work, motivated me to push onward and get them to you. For it was the messages that were my original task and learning all the rest was but an honorarium I e-motionalized, felt, and experienced with all that I am. The messages, though harsh at points, are ever so important for us to come to understand, as changes are coming in the near term. By coming to clearly understand what you are, who you have become and the potential within that Soul Being, you shall have the ability to do as you need to.

To quickly illustrate the path, or current time line of physical reality, I want to go back prior to my heart attack on the bus that morning. As I awoke that morning, I was obviously not clearly aware of the exact coming events of 9:25AM. Now, if I move back to a week, a month, or a year before, that potential time line and all its potential events still existed as something which I might have or might not have run into. A great number of elements and factors could have evolved along the way to change the outcome. It takes but a thought and a heartbeat to change a tragedy into a close call. Your knowledge of these messages becomes an element and factor that may evolve to create change within the world.

1./ *Life's Purpose*

Life's Purpose?! This is one of the greatest questions in the history of human kind. This thought-provoking and often shoulder-shrugging question has been raised throughout the duration of our history. Even after so much writing throughout the ages, this old question still remains, as its elusive answer always seems to slip around the corner just ahead of us, allowing for only a mere glimpse to know the answer is there. We're left with the impression here in the physical world that they're within our grasp, or at least to those who have written about them.

The "What am I, who am I, why am I here and what am I supposed to do with my life?" are the questions that bubble up from within at different periods during our lives. It's a seemingly simple and reasonable set of questions. But, because you were not born with a manual or some kind of guide in hand, as when purchasing a new automobile, you've gone out and bumped and banged your way through life in search of the answers. In effect, your purpose of life revolved around the searching, rather than its true intent, just as we all have done for far too long. With nearly all things in the universe being systemic in nature, this further fueled the downhill slide to a closed in, non-humanistic, societal mode of dysfunction. This in turn brings us full circle to the beginning point of asking ourselves those very same questions of what, who and why again, leading to the never-ending cycle it has been.

As though it just happened this very morning, I remember being on the *"other side"* in the presence of the four of them. The statement of life's purpose was one of only a few times in which the Teacher communicated directly to me via images. The Teacher's lesson about life's purpose was forthright in its content, being understood fully as well as acknowledged by myself without panning my attention in their direction. Once the message was received through e-motional thought form, I recounted my understanding and meaning of the relayed message. It is difficult to explain, but through an interwoven subatomic particle level with them, I felt a wave of e-motion from the Teacher, which registered images as an acceptance of that understanding.

Our task as a race of humans is but a simple one that has only been made ever so much more difficult by a lack of understanding and the outright dismissal of some of the finer aspects of your true natural Being. The reason for Being is directly connected to the purpose of life, just as the purpose of life is the reason for Being.

Life's purpose is to 1./ <u>experience</u> fully and wholly all that one can in all aspects of those experiences each individual chooses, so we can 2./ <u>learn</u> e-motionally from each and every experience, which over time allows us to 3./ <u>grow</u> more humanistic within ourselves and toward one another, in order to 4./ <u>evolve</u> at the primary Soulful level of our true initial essence and Being, to a greater state of conscious awareness of all things physical and non-physical. In simple terms, we are to Experience physically, to Learn e-motional balance, to Grow more humanistic in a Loving manner in order to Evolve to the level of the soulful Being we are.

2./ A Truth To Know

> "The Greatest ability each of us has
> is to love...
> and the greatest choice we each have
> is to use that ability"
>
> —*Alan R. Stevenson*

A specific message was relayed some time later during the session, brought forth by the Being that is a student of Teacher's and was the one closest to my left hand side. (This Being also is the first of the two white lights in the picture on the back cover.) Although gender does not exist in that dimensional realm as we perceive it in our physical reality, a distinct difference of essence is felt. As it is within our nature to differentiate due to our own physical Life experience, I felt the essence of this Being to be that of a female.

The message this Being relayed through graphical images evoked a tremendous amount of e-motion within me. That message was, "Know that you are Loved, Wanted, Needed by so many and you shall find your place to start." (The inference here of "by so many" primarily refers to those on the *"other side"* - our guides, teachers and transitioned loved ones, though it includes the people we know here in our physical lives.)

A great wave of e-motion swept over me due to the images used. The words relayed by this Being were ones I once used in a conversation with an individual. This Being's message was that I had already heard her at a different point several years before, out of need. If you should ever find yourself at a point of feeling totally lost or very chaotic within, it is for you to, at your very core, "Know that you are Loved, wanted and needed." Once you come to realize this fact to the extent that it is meant, you shall have found the proper place from which to start. This does not mean that we go back to a starting point, but instead have a new opportunity, rather than an end, each time we become lost along our journey.

It is through progress that we feel achievement, though typically it comes from the detailing of a small portion of an individual piece of the puzzle rooted within our 3D social structure. Look back over the last ten, twenty, or perhaps even forty years of your life, asking, "What have I done to fulfill the purpose of my Life?" Have you stepped through the veil of fear to experience fully and wholly, in order to learn e-motionally, so as to grow more humanistic, to have all that you are at your soul's core evolve? There are those things that truly and honestly are important, and then there are those that simply are not. It is not hard to see and more importantly, feel the difference of these opposite poles. The level at which you set your bar will determine your rate of evolution.

3./ Atomic Tie

> "Remember: That each one of us
> is an individual cell
> of the Human Race"
>
> —Alan R. Stevenson

We push a button these days to start our computers, turn a key or push a button as well to start our cars, or watch a rocket ignite and roar to the edge of space with little if any thought, other than perhaps a sense of wonder. It is no fault of yours; we are taught to simplify our existence and the physical world around us, similar to viewing a three-dimensional block, face on, simplifying it to appear as a two-dimensional square. Perhaps this is a bit of an extreme analogy, but the point is that we have been taught, for far too long to ignore the finer, more important aspects of Being as well as distracted from them. We disregard the aspects within the extended space of that square that allow us to see it for the block it is. The distraction is that we have become focused on all the things that are so very, very unimportant, while neglecting those that are. You have the choice and the ability to change that.

As you will by now have learned from the contents of this book that all things in the physical world break down to the atom as our elemental, foundational factor and beginning. Though the atom has many components to it, such as quarks, gluons, protons and neutrons, it is the electrons that are of importance. In considering the atom as that which you, I and everyone else is made of at our physical foundation, the electron is the stabilizing force in what would otherwise be an excessively chaotic state at best, assuming that matter could form at all without it.

The graphical images presented to me illustrated a finite, yet critically important connection to all things through that electrical aspect of the atom. Just as I am made of atoms, so are you and it is the atoms in between that connect us and extend to all things physical. Electrical communication lines exist between each and every one of us and it is time for us to build upon them.

We already receive the signals at times, but rarely are aware of them, unless an extreme situation presents itself. For example, you might become aware or sense at your core that someone close to you had passed, at the very moment they do, even though you are at a distance from them. Another, less obvious example is how, once in a while you have a song rolling through your mind and start to sing or hum it to yourself, only to have it already playing on the radio as we change the station.

Unfortunately, we have a tendency to brush these instances off as coincidence, rather than build upon these innate abilities we all have. Thoughts and e-motions flow through the conduit lines of atoms within us and do traverse the atoms or electrical lines between us in much the same manner. So, what flows within us, flows out and around us, affecting that which we come into contact with.

> "God's gift to each one of us
> is our abilities and talents.
> Our gift back is what we do
> with those talents and abilities."
>
> —Alan R. Stevenson

4./The Human Race Failure

> "The Opposite of Love is actually fear,
> for hate is merely the fear to Love"
>
> —Alan R. Stevenson

On the front cover, you will have perhaps noticed a vertical line intersected with a horizontal line with three smaller ones just above. The thin vertical and horizontal lines represent my time-lines during the day I died. The three smaller lines are representative of the Beings of 111, with the Teacher in the center, the female Entity to the right and the other student to the left. It was the student of the Teacher to the far left that stepped forward, becoming more prominent in the peripheral vision of my awareness to relay the next message. As this Being stepped forward I felt a wave of awe that surged throughout my true essence. This was to prepare me for the multitude of soul wrenching images that followed. Reminded by the tear that now rolls upon my cheek, the images remain clear. The first point relayed was that the Human Race is at a point of imminent failure.

Our failure begins at the singular level, due to the individual self-defeating and destructive nature we've fallen into. We have adopted a dysfunctional mode to function at all levels of being. The very acceptance of that ideology has led to the next, in which we lash out first to destroy out of fear, though we may be the one to be destroyed. This all due to the fact that we've forgotten what we are and our cohesive tie that connects us to the source of origin. By dismissing the awareness and understanding of what we are, we spend our physical lives searching for who we are. We also forget that we are an important piece of something bigger, called the Human Race.

Although in life there are no failures, only experiences from which to learn and grow, the fact remains that we are at a tipping point as the universe continually seeks to balance itself out. The simple truth is that for every in there is an out, for every up, a down and for every right there must be a left. This simple illustration helps with the understanding that for every +3 on a scale there must to be a -3 to exact a zero sum balance. Currently though, on a visual teeter-totter scale, the negative side is somewhat in an unchecked overbalance. And if you will remember, the negative side of a magnet draws and pulls to it. The time is upon us all to make a choice.

At the end of the reeling images, a rage of unfathomable sadness filled the core of my Being, spilling over and out as I asked the question, "When will we all yield to one another?" As quickly as the rage came the peaceful calmness returned. No answer was to be had, though an emotional sense came from the student in response to the question and statement I made. I realized that it is the question we all need to ask ourselves and be the first to yield with no e-motional input.

Unfortunately, we work, eat, sleep, to work again, then rinse and repeat, which has become one of the greatest contradictions in and of life, forcing us to neglect and ignore what is internally natural to us all. This creates that internal frustration that so many e-motionalize and physically feel today, yet cannot quite put their finger on. Just as the lie told often enough eventually becomes a truth, that drudgery has become a belief system. We have come so very far, yet no one - at least not enough souls - ever questioned the direction in which we were heading. We see, hear, feel and for many, experience, the direction and potential path the Human Race has a choice to take.

What is right or wrong in one culture in some part of the world may perhaps not be in another. The only common way for us all to be is that of the Loving nature we originate in and return to. The point of this is that we can get along, working together to strengthen and better humanity and the Human Race. However, we all must first get past the deeply rooted, psychological sociology we've adopted.

> "When individual cells of a body, destroy, kill, murder, and rage war upon one another within their environment, the body dies!"
>
> —*Alan R. Stevenson*

5./ *Time For Change*

> "To touch is to create an uncompromising connection"
>
> —*Alan R. Stevenson*

There is time enough to change. You now know and understand that you have the choice to change and the ability to do so through the mere purpose of your life alone. On a grander scale, though, there are so many more reasons to step out of your comfort zone and become the Being that you were always meant to be.

We have, unfortunately, accepted and adopted that defensive, closed-in sociological norm, while being unaware we were losing interest in one another along the way. A short while after the Internet first fired up, connecting the global community, I still remember thinking that I could meet and know of someone's existence in a remote place I'd otherwise never have known. What a marvel of our current history. Though it still remains a great connective tool, we have lost sight of connecting with those around us - not those individuals we already know, but the ones we do not. When was the last time you talked to someone in front or behind you while standing in a line? We stand there waiting to complete a certain objective ignoring those near to us. You have been afforded the time to make a stronger connective network of cells called Human Beings. Instead, out of fear of being rejected or ignored, we allow the time to slip away, along with a unique chance and opportunity. Once that moment has passed, the opportunity with that specific person has slipped away for ever more. Step forth as you can and should, remembering you have the right to step back and away e-motionally from the situation should it not work out. All of the moments you have are equally valuable; how you spend those coins from the palm of your hand becomes a choice only you can make.

One of the hardest facts I had to come to terms with and accept during the edification of my NDE, was that not everyone can or will be warm and fuzzy in a spiritual way. It is but a balance the universe seeks, wherein an imbalance one side or the other creates an oscillating, chaotic state throughout the universe. Remember that I mentioned back in chapter ten that the magnetic lines of a particle extend in every direction throughout the universe. One particle affects another, which affects another and so on. The end result is either a balance of the whole or an imbalanced state. Today, there are a great number of humanistic endeavors taking place globally, but we have a long way to go, to balance out the fighting, warring and killing. Healing the singular unit or body that is the Human Race begins with one cell at a time.

6./ An Epilogue...Where Are We Going

"The end is near, though not the end of all things,
but the end of a new beginning...
If we all choose to unite."

—Alan R. Stevenson

When we divide by way of gender, race or creed at an e-motional level with no focus on humanity as the end goal, we only fuel the fire to divide even more. To e-motionally and thoughtfully focus on humanity as a whole is to get to the bottom line of what we all are, and does not dismiss age, race, creed or gender. For the progression of the human race to move in a healthier direction, divisional focus must give way. Just as there are varied cultures the world over, so too are there different cells in the Human body that work together - not merely for their individual survival, but with the understanding that their survival is dependent on the whole.

On the Etch-a-Sketch board of physical reality, existence and life itself, there is little written in stone, as the equation to what is coming in the short term is continually flexing to seek a true balance. We can continue along the current path, only to have events along that path unfold as they will. Or... we can at some point soon, make a soft left or right turn on that Etch-a-Sketch board, in the end changing the picture being drawn on it.

Consider the fact, however, that in a game of chess, the most crucial mistakes are made in the last six or seven moves before a checkmate. Novice players are typically unaware they are being chased down and cornered. With the last two or three moves remaining, sometimes there is another point reached that can be referred to as an "Event Horizon". This is where the realization sets in that you are trapped. Some can think their way out of it, while others cannot change their perspective enough to see their way out, slowly being pushed into a corner.

In a roundabout way the Human Race is approaching an event horizon of its own. Where our tomorrows will lead us comes down to two tightly conjoined steps: knowing you have the ability to make a choice and using that ability. I was afforded the opportunity to learn about the Love I am of, and the Love I am from, after experiencing the pure state of Being that I know you are, too and that is how I learned to live Life after having died.

A Final Note of Thought

"Do I think this work will change the world? No, but as the seed planter that the Beings of 111 called me, I do understand this: If I could sow a thousand-acre field with acorns, the probability is that more than just one would end up sprouting. Even if only one makes it through the soil to the sunlight and that oak tree matures, seeding its own local area and those trees in time seed theirs, my task shall have been completed."